Leadership
for Kids

Curriculum for Building Intentional Leadership in Gifted Learners

Leadership
for Kids

Cecelia Boswell, Ed.D.,
Mary Christopher, Ph.D., and
JJ Colburn, M.Ed.

Routledge
Taylor & Francis Group

NEW YORK AND LONDON

Library of Congress Cataloging-in-Publication Data

Names: Boswell, Cecelia A., 1949- author. | Christopher, Mary, 1956-author.
  | Colburn, George Paul, 1970- author.
Title: Leadership for kids : curriculum for building intentional
leadership in gifted learners / by Cecelia Boswell, Ed.D., Mary Christopher, Ph.D.,
  and J. J. Colburn, M.Ed. ; edited by Katy McDowall.
Description: Waco, Texas : Prufrock Press Inc., [2018] | Includes
  bibliographical references.
Identifiers: LCCN 2017033808 | ISBN 9781618216755 (pbk.)
Subjects: LCSH: Gifted children--Education--United States. |
  Leadership--Study and teaching (Elementary) | Leadership in children.
Classification: LCC LC3993.9 .B68 2018 | DDC 371.95--dc23
LC record available at https://lccn.loc.gov/2017033808

First published in 2018 by Prufrock Press Inc.

Published in 2021 by Routledge
605 Third Avenue, New York, NY 10017
2 Park Square, Milton Park, Abingdon, Oxon OX14 4RN

Cover design by Raquel Trevino and layout design by Allegra Denbo

Routledge is an imprint of the Taylor & Francis Group, an informa business

Notice:
Product or corporate names may be trademarks or registered trademarks, and are used only
for identification and explanation without intent to infringe.

ISBN: 9781032142906 (hbk)
ISBN: 9781618216755 (pbk)

DOI: 10.4324/9781003236122

Table of Contents

Introduction

Leadership is a hot topic. Popular speakers, business and nonprofit leaders, and academic researchers tout their views of the most effective leadership styles and processes. They provide leadership training through conferences, books, webinars, retreats, and training programs. Many leaders, from CEOs, school superintendents, ministers, and university presidents, to teachers, supervisors, and managers, think that they can follow a few easy steps to become a good leader, but they may need to study leadership more intentionally. An in-depth study of leadership will guide them to develop processes and skills that help organizations function well in a variety of environments. Students, too, can benefit from development of leadership skills and perspectives.

Some gifted students appear born to lead; yet others lack the natural strengths of leadership. Just as a child exhibits gifted potential in math or language arts, he or she may also demonstrate natural tendencies to facilitate group work or organizational processes. Gifted students who possess the seeds of gifted leadership are often expected to lead because of their intellectual capacities. Educators, schools, and student organizations assume gifted students can lead because they process information well and make connections that help groups of others function well. But, as with any potentiality, gifted abilities in leadership require development. According to Bolman and Deal (2014), "Intelligence, talent, and experiences are all vital qualities for leadership, but they are not enough" (p. 3). Educators must look beyond innate gifts and nurture the skills and abilities of leaders for this millennium.

This book of activities and leadership stories guides educators as they develop leadership through a growth mindset. *Leadership for Kids* encourages classrooms where all gifted potentials, even those in leadership, are intentionally nurtured. This book will facilitate conversations about gifted children and their unique and individual needs as they develop as leaders.

DOI:10.4324/9781003236122-1

What Is Leadership?

What is your personal definition of leadership? Do good leaders give tasks and set goals so others know what to do and how to it? Do they facilitate colleagues to express ideas, set initiatives, and structure tasks? Often, the most efficient way to accomplish a task creates a situation in which followers do not take ownership of the process.

At the most basic level, leadership involves guiding a group of followers to reach a goal. But it is so much more. Experts and popular speakers in the field elicit several perspectives that might inform the definition of leadership. In his 2001 book, *Good to Great*, Jim Collins outlined a Level 5 leader as one who builds enduring greatness through a paradoxical blend of personal humility and professional will. As organizations move from "good" to "great," they must develop Level 5 leaders. Sheryl Sandberg, chief operating officer for Facebook and founder of Lean In, views leadership from the perspective of a woman who worked in a competitive business community for many years. Sandberg (2013) defined leadership as "making others better as a result of your presence and making sure that impact lasts in your absence" (p. 293). Brene Brown (2012), a research professor in social work, presented a unique view of leadership: "Leadership has nothing to do with position, salary, or number of direct reports. I believe a leader is anyone who holds herself or himself accountable for finding potential in people and processes" (para. 1). Steven Covey (2004), a well-known expert, developed his definition of leadership through his dissertation study. He defined leadership as "communicating to people their worth and potential so clearly that they are inspired to see it in themselves" (p. 216). Warren Bennis and Robert Townsend (2005), pioneers in the contemporary study of leadership, defined leadership as "the capacity to translate vision into reality" (p. 143).

Another approach to leadership development focuses on using different views of leadership to solve problems and call others to action. Bolman and Deal (2014), respected professors and authors, have studied leadership for most of their professional careers. They call leaders to *reframe* or look at things from different perspectives to develop a clear vision to achieve results. Through reframing, leaders move from reacting to conflict to using their strengths to respond to challenging situations as they become intentional leaders. The authors' four frames (structural, human resource, political, and symbolic) create new perspectives that allow leaders to understand their setting and set a direction for organizations that may be both innovative and powerful.

So where does that leave you? How would you define leadership? Take a few minutes to consider the essentials that support effective leadership. What characteristics, skills, and perspective of leadership do your students need to study so that they can become intentional leaders?

Leadership Traits

Strong, effective leaders exhibit common traits that facilitate organizational functions and processes. The United States Marine Corps highlighted 14 leadership traits that help Marines earn respect, confidence, and loyalty as they lead fellow Marines. These traits are justice, judgment, dependability, initiative, decisiveness, tact, integrity, enthusiasm, bearing, unselfishness, courage, knowledge, loyalty, and endurance (Hurt, 2013). Prive (2012), CEO of CoFoundersLab, created a list of 10 qualities that make great leaders, particularly great entrepreneurs. She called for leaders to model honesty and ethical behavior, delegate tasks according to team members' strengths, communicate clearly, stay confident and calm, remain committed to the brand and their role, motivate team members to remain positive, use creative thinking to solve problems, guide through intuition, inspire the team to reach goals, and customize their approach to individuals.

Although these and many other lists of traits provide a productive background to understand the concept of leadership, two academic perspectives provide a valid approach to understanding leadership traits. Giles (2016) collected data to determine particular characteristics and behaviors used by effective leaders. Kirkpatrick and Locke (1991) reviewed the literature and categorized several traits that support leadership skill development.

Giles (2016) researched 195 leaders in 15 countries to determine their priorities of the most important leadership competencies. She grouped the top 10 competencies in five themes: (1) strong ethics and safety, (2) self-organization, (3) efficient learning, (4) nurtured growth, and (5) connection and belonging. The first category combines several competencies that include "high ethical and moral standards" and "communicating clear expectations" (para. 2). These traits create an environment in which followers feel safe, freeing them for creativity and innovation. The theme of self-organizing describes leaders who empower team members to organize their own time and tasks to accomplish goals. Efficient learning supports a culture of openness, flexibility, and risk-taking that allows team members to approach new ideas without fear of failure. By demonstrating openness to learning within themselves, leaders encourage similar behaviors in their followers. Effective leaders nurture growth through mentoring and ongoing learning, which provide more success in their followers. In this setting, followers naturally tend to express gratitude and feel less stress. Leaders who communicate often and openly create a strong sense of belonging and connection. Members who feel valued as part of the team experience increased productivity and well-being.

Kirkpatrick and Locke (1991) outlined the ways leaders differ from nonleaders. The six traits include "drive, the desire to lead, honesty/integrity, self-confidence, cognitive ability, and knowledge of business" (p. 49). Drive involves the motivation, tenacity, and initiative to push forward ideas and innovations. Effective leaders enjoy completing challenging tasks and projects that improve the organization or the products. Because leaders cannot accomplish tasks alone, they want and need to lead others. Their motivation comes from guiding others while gaining authority and assuming responsibility. As leaders gain power, they also empower others in the organization. Several experts support the need for leaders to demonstrate honesty and integrity. "Honesty is absolutely essential to leadership. . . . We want to know that he or she is being truthful, ethical and principled. We want to be fully confident in the integrity of our leaders" (Kouzes & Posner, 1995, p. 122). Student leaders appear more trustworthy and reliable than followers do (Bass & Stogdill, 1990). Leaders must maintain self-confidence when making decisions, facing difficulties, and implementing initiatives. Even when initiatives fail, strong leaders foster self-confidence in their followers when they take responsibility for the failures and use them as a learning opportunity. Effective leaders must be intelligent and skilled in order to "formulate suitable strategies, solve problems, and make correct decisions" (Kirkpatrick & Locke, 1991, p. 55) in a rapidly changing world. Good judgment and strategic thinking demonstrate reasoning ability needed by competent leaders. Leaders hold an in-depth knowledge of the organization they lead. This knowledge may include formal education but more likely focuses on organization-specific experiences.

The various leadership traits described above provide only the potential for leadership. This potential may be actualized through the development of skills for decision making, problem solving, and performance appraisal. A well-articulated vision implemented effectively demonstrates the ultimate realization of the leader's potential. According to Kirckpatrick and Locke (1991), "Leaders do not have to be great men or women by being intellectual geniuses or omniscient prophets to succeed, but they do need to have the 'right stuff' and this stuff is not equally present in all people" (p. 58).

Rationale for Developing Leadership in Gifted Students

Beginning with the Marland Report (1972), education experts and organizations included leadership in most definitions of giftedness. This report served as a watershed moment in gifted education in the United States, calling for appropriate services for this special population in six areas. Marland and his committee viewed leadership as an integral aspect of giftedness:

> Gifted and talented children are those identified by professionally qualified persons who by virtue of outstanding abilities, are capable of high performance. These are children who require differentiated educational programs and/or services beyond those normally pro-

vided by the regular school program in order to realize their contribution to self and society. Children capable of high performance include those with demonstrated achievement and/or potential ability in any of the following areas, singly or in combination:

1. general intellectual ability
2. specific academic aptitude
3. creative or productive thinking
4. leadership ability
5. visual and performing arts
6. psychomotor ability. (p. ix)

Since that time, many states and professional organizations refined definitions to fit the latest trends in research and professional practice. The current federal definition (Javits, 1988) follows a similar approach to the Marland Report with a more direct focus on the development of gifted capabilities. The National Association for Gifted Children (NAGC, 2010) redefined giftedness to focus on the development of ability or talent:

Gifted individuals are those who demonstrate outstanding levels of aptitude (defined as exceptional ability to reason and learn) or competence (documented performance or achievement in top 10% or rarer) in one or more domains. Domains include any structure area of activity with its own symbol system (e.g., mathematics, music, language) and/or set of sensorimotor skills (e.g., painting, dance, and sports).

The development of ability or talent is a lifelong process. It can be evident in young children as exceptional performance on tests and/or other measures of ability or as a rapid rate of learning, compared to other students of the same age, or in actual achievement in a domain. As individuals mature through childhood to adolescence, however, achievement and high levels of motivation in the domain become the primary characteristics of their giftedness. Various factors can either enhance or inhibit the development and expression of abilities. (p. 1)

Although NAGC (2010) did not include leadership explicitly in the definition, the concept of ability/talent development of the student's particular areas of strength should encompass leadership as well.

According to Texas Education Code §29.121 (1995),

gifted and talented student means a child or youth who performs at or shows the potential for performing at a remarkably high level of accomplishment when compared to others of the same age, experience, or environment and who: (1) exhibits high performance capability in an intellectual, creative, or artistic area; (2) possesses an unusual capacity for leadership; or (3) excels in a specific academic field.

The inclusion of leadership in the definition highlights the expectation that students can exhibit strengths in this area, although districts are not required to identify or serve in all areas of giftedness mentioned in the definition.

A review of state definitions reveals limited specificity in particular areas of giftedness, but approximately one third of them include leadership as a potential area of strength (e.g., California, Colorado, Iowa, Maryland, and Minnesota). Even those states that do not specifically state leadership as an area of gifted potential list outstanding abilities that require services not usually provided in the school program. Regardless of the inclusion or exclusion of leadership in definitions of giftedness, most gifted programs focus on academic, intellectual, and creative development. According to Matthews (2004), "Leadership remains the least served of the domains of giftedness" (p. 78). Therefore, gifted students with leadership potential often are not identified or served within the gifted program in a school.

The definitions listed above help educators focus on gifted students' potential in particular areas, including leadership, but schools must consider the intentional development of leadership as well. Individuals who demonstrate strength and interest in leadership hold natural gifts that must be cultivated. Current trends in the business, military, government, sports, and professional communities highlight the importance of developing leaders (Karnes & Bean, 2010). These organizations select young leaders and provide intensive, ongoing training to support the development of their leadership potential. They rely on leaders who not only manage others well but also provide the vision, political insight, and relational skills to guide the organization in an effective, ethical manner. As society becomes more collaborative, the development of emerging leaders becomes more important. Gifted learners who show leadership capabilities and potential must be prepared to serve as the next generation of leaders. They may not reach their leadership potential without "challenging learning experiences that instill creative and critical thinking" (Leshnower, 2008, p. 29) supporting effective leadership.

Gifted students are often described as future leaders at community, state, national, and global levels. Educators assume that the development of advanced knowledge and expertise in a particular area will provide the necessary background for gifted students to move into leadership roles. If gifted students do not also develop leadership skills and perspectives, however, these gifted individuals may not lead well. Recent research supports the ideas that leadership is something that can and must be developed (Karnes & Bean, 2010). Most people influence others, but the development of gifted leaders rests in guiding them to influence others in positive rather than negative ways. Future leaders will face complex challenges as creators, empathizers, pattern recognizers, and meaning makers (Pink, 2006). Gifted individuals exhibit some of these strengths by nature, but educators need to intentionally develop leadership potential in gifted students at an early age. Educators must guide and develop those individuals who possess gifts in leadership to help society accomplish great things (Nelson, 2016).

Common Models of Leadership

The classic *Handbook of Leadership* (Bass & Stogdill, 1990) outlined an extensive list of leadership models and serves as the seminal book on the subject. Because of the complexity of leadership study, current educators often focus on a limited scope of common models to study, such as transactional, transformational, and servant leadership. A clear understanding of these models of leadership will enhance the study of leadership.

Transactional leaders "approach followers with an eye to exchange one thing for another" (Bass & Stogdill, 1990, p. 41). The followers seek to obey the leader who motivates through formal authority and organizational responsibility. Through a system of rewards and punishment, the leader and followers achieve performance goals. Rather than being self-motivated, the subordinates are closely monitored and controlled. This efficient model gets work done but limits the creativity of members of the group. Issues emerge from this model because the leaders are preoccupied with power and position rather than motivation and growth.

Transformational leadership, developed by Burns (1978), focuses on creating positive change in the followers. The leader seeks to raise the followers to higher levels of motivation, values, and performance. These leaders empower employees or group members to achieve goals by appealing to ideals and values. They set a mission and goals while encouraging others to put these group goals above their own. The transformational leader seeks to "satisfy higher needs" of the follower (Bass & Stogdill, 1990, p. 41) in terms of Maslow's (1954) hierarchy of needs, which results in self-actualization. The four components of transformational leadership include charisma, inspirational motivation, intellectual stimulation, and individual attention. In this model, both leaders and followers grow to become "intellectual leaders, leaders of reform or revolution, and heroes or ideologues" (Bass & Stogdill, 1990, p. 41).

The Servant Leadership Model (Greenleaf, 1979) focuses on converting followers into leaders, allowing the leader to be one among many. The needs of others become the leader's highest priority as he or she becomes a servant who builds relationships with his or her followers (Bass & Stogdill, 1990). The leader, as servant first, shows others the way to reach the goals by building trust and confidence. Although the followers are being served, they become healthier, wiser, freer, more autonomous, and likely to become servants as well (Greenleaf, 1979). These models offer characteristics and positive actions for leaders, but they do not address how to lead by understanding the needs of the group, analyzing situations to address a variety of issues, and focusing on the particular needs of an organization. Particular frames of leadership provide a better focus for this analysis and action (Bolman & Deal, 2014).

Reframing Leadership

For more than 40 years, Bolman and Deal (2014) have studied and written about organizational leadership. As consultants and professors at several universities, including Harvard, they found common interest in helping guide leaders to negotiate change and solve problems by reframing their thinking. Although most leadership programs focus on leadership styles, models, and actions, Bolman and Deal emphasized thinking that needs to precede action. Otherwise, leaders' actions involve mindless decisions with little clear direction. These decisions may work initially but often do not stand the test of time. Using the structural, human resource, political, and symbolic frames, leaders analyze the situation and set a course for organizations, both large and small.

Bolman and Deal (2014) provided effective tools to help leaders reframe their thinking and develop a revised picture of their setting to facilitate effective functioning of the group or team. Leaders in many organizations find success following the latest leadership trend, only to find the business or organization falling into difficulties in the coming years. These bright people do not fail because of lack of abilities, but a lack of thinking through things in a comprehensive view. They hold a limited view of the situation and construct their own meaning. Use of the four frames of leadership encourages them to move beyond this limited view to see what is happening, consider more options, and make better choices.

A frame involves "a set of beliefs and assumptions that you carry in your head to help you understand and negotiate some part of your world" (Bolman & Deal, 2014, p. 11). The structural, human resource, political, and symbolic frames allow people to gather information through observation, data collection, and experiences to create an overview of a particular situation. Although individuals naturally view the world through a particular paradigm, mindset, or frame, they need to shift frames when the circumstances change. Reframing requires breaking those natural tendencies in order to consider new perspectives or viewpoints. Leading a group, business, or organization is hard work that requires time, effort, practice, and feedback. Understanding the four frames over time helps leaders develop the expertise to lead with confidence and skill.

Leadership Orientation Within the Four Frames

Most people work more comfortably within a particular frame. When confronted with a conflict or problem, the first inclination is to lead out of their strength. For example, a leader with strengths in the structural frame naturally sets goals and assigns tasks to accomplish those goals. A leader with strengths in the symbolic frame easily sets the vision and calls people to action. Although leaders need to think through the four frames as they solve problems and manage groups, they often begin with a narrower vision. They need to balance their leadership preferences through the development of the other frames or surround themselves with other leaders with different leadership preferences. Bolman and Deal (2014) developed a Leadership Orientation survey to help individuals assess their leadership preferences. The results are measured and plotted on a four-dimensional grid to form a leadership "kite."

Structure of the Book

The following sections of the book fulfill several purposes. After the introductory lessons introducing students to leadership, each section begins with an explanation of a particular frame to help students understand Bolman and Deal's (2014) unique view of leadership. Their frames filter the wealth of ideas on leadership and capture the subtlety and complexity of leadership in a simple, understandable structure. Following each explanation, several activities guide students in the development of the individual frames of leadership. The first activity in each section clarifies the frame through active learning in which students use the frame to complete a particular task. In the remaining activities, students use the frames to solve problems, collaborate with other students, develop structure, and call others to action.

The final chapter of the book includes leader stories demonstrating the use of one or more of the frames. People share their life experiences through stories. When leaders share their stories, others learn from their experiences, both good and bad. Analyzing the leader stories through the frames helps other leaders think in new ways to solve problem and manage organizations. These stories and the accompanying activity serve as a culmination to the study of intentional leadership through the four frames. Teachers and students can synthesize and apply their understanding of intentional leadership through this culminating activity.

Lesson 1

Looking at Leadership

Objectives

In this lesson, students will:
- develop a definition of leadership,
- determine characteristics of leadership, and
- describe examples and nonexamples of leadership.

Guiding Questions

- What does leadership look like?
- What are some actions of leaders?

Materials

- Handout 1: Looking at Leadership
- Crayons, colored pencils, or other writing utensils for students
- Whiteboard, flipchart, or SmartBoard for discussion

Getting Started

This lesson establishes students' basic understanding of leadership and leaders.

Activity

1. Distribute Handout 1: Looking at Leadership. The handout includes a Frayer Model to help students synthesize their definition of *leadership* by first listing characteristics, examples, and nonexamples of leadership. Tell students that there are no right or wrong answers because the goal is to learn about their understanding of leadership. They can list or draw their responses. Provide students with 15–20 minutes to complete the handout. They should take the time to think of their ideas, add to their original thoughts, and add anything they feel is relevant.

2. As students complete the activity, have them display their handouts around the room. In a gallery walk, have students move around the room reading each other's responses. As they view other students' work, have students take

DOI:10.4324/9781003236122-2

notes of ideas they would like to add to their handout or questions they would like to ask others.

3. **Talk about it:** Afterward, ask students if they have any new ideas about leaders and leadership. Ask:
   ◇ Do leaders always know what is best for the group?
   ◇ How did the nonexamples help you think about the characteristics of leaders and leadership?
   ◇ Did the examples you saw from others match your examples?
   ◇ Did you see new characteristics that you hadn't thought about?

Assessment

This activity preassesses the students' prior knowledge. Use the information as a starting point for development of *intentional leadership*. This preassessment provides a baseline of students' understanding of characteristics of leaders and of leadership.

Variation

After the gallery walk:
- Ask students to categorize the whole group's examples of leadership. Using the list, ask students to develop categories. For example, categories might be "collaborate" or "dictates."
- Group students in threes to develop their definition of leadership based on the categories created by the whole group.

Looking at Leadership

Directions: Complete the organizer. List and/or draw at least three characteristics of leadership as well as at least three examples and nonexamples of leadership. Then, provide your definition of *leadership*.

Characteristics of Leadership	**Examples of Leadership**

Leadership

Nonexamples of Leadership	**Definition of Leadership**

Lesson 2

Defining Leadership

Objectives

In this lesson, students will:
- ♦ refine their definition of leadership, and
- ♦ compare their definition with that of their peers.

Guiding Questions

- ♦ What does leadership look like in your peers?
- ♦ What are some examples in peers that you could adopt or adapt?

Materials

- ♦ Handout 2: Refining Leadership
- ♦ Whiteboard, flipchart, or SmartBoard for discussion

Getting Started

This lesson starts the process of students' thinking not only about their definition of leadership but also about how others define and exhibit it. By asking students to think about their thinking (metacognition), they can begin to explore a variety of leadership characteristics, which serves as the basis for their learning in this book.

Activity

1. Have students work individually and write down their responses. Ask them to list three students that they know who fit their definition of leadership. Then, have them list and describe qualities the other students demonstrate that they would like to develop or enhance in themselves and why.

2. Divide students into groups of two or three, and distribute Handout 2: Refining Leadership. Each group will describe one female and one male leader and prepare to act out each characteristic for classmates to guess whom they selected. Tell students to select leaders who will be known to their classmates, such as presidents, governors, famous entertainers (singers, actors, television personalities), cartoon characters, or local government officials.

DOI:10.4324/9781003236122-3

3. **Talk about it:** Lead a follow-up discussion, and ask students to compare and contrast leadership characteristics of their male or female choice.

Assessment

No formal assessment will follow this activity. Read students' written responses to ensure they understand the concept of leadership.

Variation

Have students act out characteristics they found in their leader.

Refining Leadership

Directions: Think of one female and one male leader. List three characteristics of each. Be ready to act out each one for classmates to guess whom you selected. Compare the leadership characteristics of each. Be ready to answer, "What are their similarities? What are their differences?"

Female: _____	Male: _____

Lesson 3

Eminent Leadership

Objective

In this lesson, students will express their understanding of leadership as observed in prominent people they perceive as leaders.

Guiding Questions

◆ Who are leaders?
◆ How can leadership be categorized?
◆ In what way(s) is celebrity different from or the same as leadership?

Materials

◆ Handout 3: Categorizing Leaders
◆ Crayons, colored pencils, or other writing utensils for students

Getting Started

This lesson asks students to observe leadership in their town/city, their county, their state, or the world. Students will consider the term *celebrity* and its relation to leadership.

Activity

1. Guide students through examples of leadership from local and national news-papers, magazines, online searches, biographies and autobiographies, TED talks, and any sources that are specific to celebrity and to leadership.
2. After a guided discussion about leaders across the spectrum, distribute Handout 3: Categorizing Leaders. Students will research leaders and place their choices in the following categories: *famous/infamous*, *factual/fictional*, and *past/present*. They will also develop their own categories.
3. Upon completion of their chart, have students select one example to present to the class with justification for their choice and categorization.

DOI:10.4324/9781003236122-4

4. **Talk about it:** After students present, lead a discussion based on their examples about what makes or does not make a leader a celebrity. Also, discuss what does or does not make a celebrity a leader.

Assessment

Evaluate students' work using a rubric that fits your students' needs. Suggested resources include:

- RubiStar (http://rubistar.4teachers.org/index.php)
- Texas Performance Standards Project (http://www.texaspsp.org/intermediate/assessment/Intermediate_Rubric.pdf)
- Rubrics by Exemplars (http://www.exemplars.com/resources/rubrics)
- Common Core State Standards Writing Rubric by School Improvement Network (http://www.schoolimprovement.com/common-core-standards-writing-rubric)
- K–12 Rubrics by Elk Grove Unified School District (http://blogs.egusd.net/ccss/educators/ela/rubrics-k-12)
- Grading and Performance Rubrics by Eberly Center (https://www.cmu.edu/teaching/designteach/teach/rubrics.html)

Variation

Allow students to present through a means of their choice.

Categorizing Leaders

Directions: Complete these charts with at least two examples of each. Select two of your own categories on the last chart. First, list the leader's name. Then, place a checkmark under the category that best fits that person. Then, place a checkmark to describe if the person is a celebrity, a leader, or both.

Famous or Infamous?

Leader's Name	Famous	Infamous	Celebrity	Leader

Factual or Fictional?

Leader's Name	Factual	Fictional	Celebrity	Leader

Handout 3, Continued.

Past or Present?

Leader's Name	Past	Present	Celebrity	Leader

Your Categories

Leader's Name	_____	_____	Celebrity	Leader

Select one of the examples to present to the class. Include in your presentation why you chose the person and justify why you believe the person to be a celebrity, a leader, or both.

Finding Leadership

Objectives

In this lesson, students will:

- ◆ connect their definition of leadership to their experiences, and
- ◆ illustrate their examples.

Guiding Questions

- ◆ What does leadership look like in a story or game?
- ◆ How do movies, television shows, or games portray leadership?

Materials

- ◆ Handout 4: Leadership in Media
- ◆ Crayons, colored pencils, or other writing utensils for students

Getting Started

This lesson introduces students to the idea that leadership occurs in all venues. The activity asks students to illustrate leadership in a story line or game of their choice. By connecting leadership to a movie, television show, or game, students use examples from their experiences. (*Note.* Although Follow the Leader is an example of a game, encourage students to go beyond the obvious.)

Activity

1. Ask students to think about movies they know, television shows they watch, or games they play that show leadership. Give them 3 minutes to think to themselves before answering. Next, as a class, brainstorm a list of movies, television shows, or games. As in any brainstorming session, reserve judgment about students' choices.
2. Distribute Handout 4: Leadership in Media for students to complete. As students complete the activity, they may choose from the class list, but are not limited to it.

DOI:10.4324/9781003236122-5

3. **Talk about it:** Let students explain their drawings or descriptions or create a gallery walk.

Assessment

When students have completed the activity and explained examples, use a discussion circle to evaluate examples of leadership. Give participation grades.

Teacher's Note. A discussion circle is a version of Socratic Seminar. Arrange two rings of chairs, an outer ring and an inner ring. Students may choose to be in either ring. Students on the outer ring will only listen to the discussion. They may make notes to be used later. Students in the inner ring will discuss their example of entertainment venue using an open-ended question starter. The teacher should create the questions for the first discussion. Students should ultimately create their own question starter, such as "In what ways does entertainment portray leadership? Provide examples."

After a set amount of time, as determined by the teacher, the students in the outer ring may switch roles with the inner ring, or individual students in the outer ring may ask to trade with a student in the inner ring in order to express their thoughts to the group.

HANDOUT 4

Leadership in Media

Directions: List three of your favorite movies, television shows, and/or games.

1.

2.

3.

Which have an example of leadership within the story line?

Choose one of your three. Draw or describe it below.

Lesson 5

Thoughts on Leadership

Objectives

In this lesson, students will express their understanding of leadership.

Guiding Questions

- ◆ Who are leaders?
- ◆ What is leadership?

Materials

- ◆ Handout 5: Thoughts on Leadership
- ◆ Crayons, colored pencils, or other writing utensils for students

Guiding Principles

Before students begin the study of the leadership frames, they must develop a concept of leadership that is concrete and relevant to them.

Activity

1. **Talk about it:** Guide students through a review of the leadership activities they have completed. Allow them to use all of their previous work and anything you have posted as a reference for this activity.
2. Have students create an original short story, poem, essay, song, or drawing (with an oral or written explanation) that illustrates their understanding of leadership. You may determine the length of time they have to complete this activity.

Assessment

Evaluate students' work using a rubric that fits your students' needs (see Lesson 3 for suggested resources).

Variation

Provide students with options of additional acceptable projects from which to choose, such as those listed at http://www.bertiekingore.com/PortfolioProducts.pdf.

DOI:10.4324/9781003236122-6

HANDOUT 5

Thoughts on Leadership

Directions: Write a short story, poem, essay, song, or drawing based on your understanding of leadership. Jot down ideas you have about leadership on this graphic before staring your work.

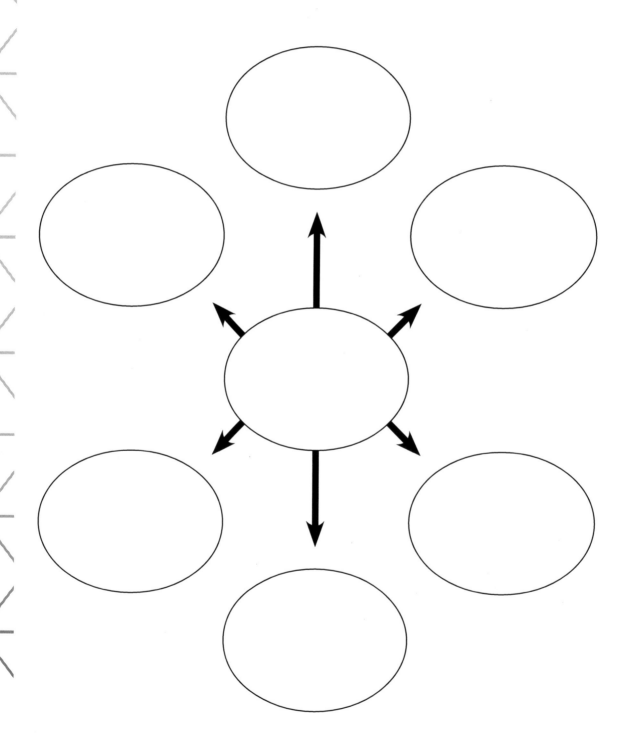

Lesson 6

Leadership Orientation

Objectives

In this lesson, students will:
- complete the leadership orientation, and
- score it to determine their leadership preferences.

Guiding Questions

- How do *you* lead?
- What describes you as a leader?

Materials

- "Frames Quick Self-Rating Scale" (available at http://www.bolman.com/frames_selfrating_scale.htm)
- Student computer and Internet access

Getting Started

Effective instructional practice begins with preassessment. Because most leaders feel comfortable leading out of one to two frames, you may want to determine each student's natural strengths in particular frames. Prior to beginning the study of Bolman and Deal's (2014) leadership frames, students would benefit from completing the "Frames Quick Self-Rating Scale" to determine their leadership preferences. Then, as they study leadership from the four frames, they can learn how to use all four frames as needed in a particular group setting or to solve a particular problem.

Activity

1. Have students take the free, self-scoring online version of the "Frames Self-Rating Scale" (see Materials list) to assess their leadership preferences and create their own leadership "kite."
2. Have students refer to this information as they learn about the four frames and complete the activities in the following chapters.

DOI:10.4324/9781003236122-7

Chapter 1

The Structural Frame

❏   Do you set a goal when trying to solve a problem?

❏   Do you like to draw or make a list of ideas before making a decision?

❏   Do you lead by first thinking about options for the solution?

If so, you may prefer to lead from a structural frame.

The structural frame bases decisions on reason, rationality, and structure. Persons who lead from the structural frame focus on setting goals, creating policies, designing specialized roles, using technology, coordinating teams, and maintaining formal relationships. These efforts coordinate diverse activities to support a unified effort within a particular organizational environment. Bolman and Deal (2014) used the metaphor of a factory to typify the structural frame. Just as a factory needs structure and particular roles to complete a product, a leader using the structural frame creates a workable environment to accomplish tasks. Great structural leaders share several characteristics. They

- ◆ prepare effectively;
- ◆ insist on clear goals;
- ◆ rethink the relationship of structure, strategy, and environment;
- ◆ focus on detail and implementation; and
- ◆ experiment (p. 21).

When structure is in place, organizations function more effectively. Rather than providing a structure that is rigid and confining, the structural frame provides pro-

DOI:10.4324/9781003236122-8

ductivity and satisfaction. Creating a social architecture within a particular context involves understanding the situation and designing a structure that helps the organization function. Stable environments use simple structures with well-defined goals and often use top-down strategies. Complex environments require flexible structures with decentralized strategies. Changes in the workforce may create a need for specialized roles and more discretion in daily tasks. A few simple questions can guide structural analysis through this frame (Bolman & Deal, 2014):

- What is going on? What is working and not working?
- What is changing (in our organization, our technology, or your environment) that creates an opportunity, a threat, or both?
- What problem do you need to solve? What options should you consider? (p. 32)

Although people who lead from the structural frame help groups to function well, they may overlook human emotions, political issues, and cultural bonds. They may risk working as rigid micromanagers who limit the strengths that other frames bring to leadership.

Lesson 7

Alphabet Sound-Off

Objectives

In this lesson, students will:
- develop a plan to achieve a goal, and
- listen to others to brainstorm solutions to a problem.

Guiding Questions

- Why is it important for leaders using the structural frame to develop a plan?
- How do leaders using the structural frame listen to others to solve problems?

Materials

There are no materials needed for this lesson.

Getting Started

The structural frame uses effective listening techniques with stakeholders to help develop and execute a plan. Two of the things leaders who use the structural frame do are set goals and coordinate teams. The activity in this lesson guides students to practice leading from the structural frame by developing an effective plan.

Activity

1. Tell students: *Your goal today is to say the alphabet out loud, one student at a time, with your eyes closed. Seems easy to accomplish, doesn't it? But there are some special rules:*
   ◇ Do not talk to each other prior to beginning this task or during the task, except to say the letters.
   ◇ Spread throughout the room so that you are spaced evenly.
   ◇ Close your eyes and keep them closed.
   ◇ Each person must participate in this activity by saying at least one letter. If you get to the end of the alphabet and everyone has not spoken, start at the beginning of the alphabet again.

DOI:10.4324/9781003236122-9

◇ A person can say more than one letter as long as they are not consecutive (i.e., one person saying E, F, and G in a row).

◇ Anytime two people say a letter at the same time, the group must start the task again.

2. **Talk about it:** Ask students:

◇ What made the task difficult without making a plan?

◇ During the first attempts, did you develop some ideas to determine when to speak?

◇ How did you feel when the group was not successful with the task?

◇ What behaviors did you use to contribute to the group's success?

3. After developing a plan, repeat the activity. When the group has successfully met the goal, follow up with a discussion of the difference between the two attempts. Consider the experience of setting a plan to achieve a goal using the structural frame.

4. **Talk about it:** Ask students: *What did you learn about goal setting and listening from this activity?*

Assessment

Use informal assessment during the discussion to determine if students understand the use of goal setting and listening in the structural frame. Follow up with open-ended questions in areas that you determine the students have not mastered.

Lesson 8

The Gist of Structural Leadership

Objectives

In this lesson, students will:
- identify keywords and phrases related to structural leadership, and
- write a description of structural leadership.

Guiding Questions

- What does a leader look like who works from a structural frame?
- What are some actions of a leader who works from a structural frame?

Materials

- Handout 8: Keywords
- Crayons, colored pencils, or other writing utensils for students
- Whiteboard, flipchart, or SmartBoard for discussion

Getting Started

This activity helps familiarize students with the terms related to the structural frame.

Activity

1. Introduce students to the structural frame. Read aloud the description on pp. 27–28.
2. Handout 8: Keywords asks students to list at least 20 keywords and/or phrases from the description. From their list, students should synthesize their words and phrases into a definition of the structural frame of leadership using at least 20 words.
3. **Talk about it:** Have students read their sentences aloud. Listeners should check off all of the words they hear that are the same as theirs.

DOI:10.4324/9781003236122-10

Assessment

This activity familiarizes students with the structural frame of leadership. No grades should be assigned.

Variation

Students could list their words on a collective poster and create their sentences as a group.

Keywords

Directions: Structural leaders base decisions on reason, rationality, and structure. Based on your understanding of the structural frame, list or draw keywords and phrases that describe this type of leader. Then, write a 20-word sentence using as many of your keywords or phrases as you can to describe a structural leader.

Keywords or Phrases:

A 20-Word Sentence:

Lesson 9

Bookmarking

Objectives

In this lesson, students will:
◆ discuss the frame of a structural leader, and
◆ provide examples and nonexamples of a structural leader.

Guiding Questions

◆ What does structural leadership look like?
◆ What are some actions of structural leaders?

Materials

◆ Handout 9: Bookmarking the Structural Frame
◆ Crayons, colored pencils, or other writing utensils for students
◆ Whiteboard, flipchart, or SmartBoard for discussion

Getting Started

Using the characteristics of the structural frame, students will create a bookmark as a reference tool. You may use the included handout or encourage students to create their own bookmark.

Activity

1. Distribute Handout 9: Bookmarking the Structural Frame. Students will create bookmarks to remind them of the main characteristics of the structural frame. They may write or draw their ideas. Students should cut out their bookmarks for future reference, but they should not write their names on the bookmarks just yet.
2. **Talk about it:** Collect the bookmarks, then have students trade bookmarks. Let them guess whose bookmark they have and why they think so.
3. Afterward, ask students to retrieve their own bookmark and write their name on the back.

DOI:10.4324/9781003236122-11

Teacher's Note. Consider laminating students' bookmarks for safekeeping.

Assessment

It is not important to assess this activity because there is not a defined answer. Ask students to determine how they would grade the bookmark. Their ideas may be used in a future assessment.

Variation

Introduce students to the bookmarks in their web browsers. Let them brainstorm ways to use this type of bookmark with this activity.

Name:_____ Date: _____

Bookmarking the Structural Frame

Directions: Create a bookmark to remind you of the main characteristics of the frame a structural leader uses. You may write or draw your ideas. Then, cut out your bookmark so you can keep it for reference. Do *not* write your name on your bookmark until your teacher asks you to.

© Taylor & Francis Group • *Leadership for Kids*

Lesson 10

Problem Solving

Objectives

In this lesson, students will:
- determine characteristics of leaders using the structural frame, and
- solve a problem as a leader using the structural frame would.

Guiding Questions

- How does the structural frame guide a leader?
- How do leaders using the structural frame respond to problems?

Materials

- Handout 10: The First Day of School
- Crayons, colored pencils, or other writing utensils for students

Getting Started

The structural frame addresses leaders who are social architects. They analyze a situation and design a plan to solve an issue or problem. Through this lesson, students should understand that this type of leader likes to experiment with ideas and adapt the situation so that the issue or problem may be solved. This leader focuses on the environment surrounding the situation and uses strategy and structure to address the issue or problem.

Activity

1. Review the characteristics of the structural frame.
2. Distribute Handout 10: The First Day of School for students to complete.
3. **Talk about it:** Afterward, ask students to discuss their T-charts from the handout to collectively structure a solution. Then, have students discuss any new ideas they have about structural leadership.

DOI:10.4324/9781003236122-12

The First Day of School

Directions: In your school, students may participate in the following activities in addition to the regular schoolwork:

♦ a local spelling bee that leads to a state and national winner,

♦ the local school's reading contest,

♦ basketball or baseball/softball, and

♦ music/band.

Two students from Uzbekistan enroll in your grade. Sasha and Sergei speak their home language but can read and write some English. They do not speak English very well but seem to understand what is being said. They get along with everyone and have fun working and playing with all students.

The school requires that students sign up for the extracurricular options listed above within 3 days of school beginning. Practicing the structural frame of leadership, help the new students decide what activity or activities they will select.

Using the following chart, write what you know and what you would like to know about the new students to help solve their problem. Remember: You are solving the issue as a structural leader.

What I Know About Sasha	What I Want to Know About Sasha

What I Know About Sergei	What I Want to Know About Sergei

Lesson 11

Free Play

Objectives

In this lesson, students will:
- ◆ set goals for solving a problem, and
- ◆ use the structural frame to practice leadership in this activity.

Guiding Questions

- ◆ What goals should be determined to solve a problem in the structural frame?
- ◆ What details will be required to solve the problem in the structural frame?

Materials

- ◆ Handout 11: Free Play
- ◆ Sticky notes
- ◆ Padlet (http://www.padlet.com; optional)

Getting Started

Leaders using the structural frame set clear goals, focus on details and implementation, and experiment with ideas. In this lesson, students will use their skills within the structural frame to solve another problem. In order to make sure that everyone contributes to the solution, use a bulletin board to place all ideas on sticky notes or use Padlet if available.

Activity

1. Distribute Handout 11: Free Play for students to complete.
2. **Talk about it:** Students will convince the teacher that the *cons* are really *pros*. This discussion helps students focus on details and implementation as well as use their evaluative thinking ability. Ensure that students have written or drawn their details and steps in implementation. Their evaluative skills will come as they rethink their solutions to see another viewpoint. The purpose is not only to be able to relay their original thinking and work, but also to

DOI:10.4324/9781003236122-13

be able to see other ways of looking at the situation, as well as other possible solutions.

Assessment

Ask students to respond to the following question through a format of your choice: *What details did you list for the principal, and why did you choose those details?*

Variation

If available, complete the activity using only Padlet.

HANDOUT 11

Free Play

Directions: Leaders who use the structural frame set clear goals, focus on details and implementation, and experiment with ideas. Use your skills using the structural frame to solve this problem.

For many years, all students had 30 minutes after lunch for free play. Five years ago a student was severely injured during this time. Instead of free play after lunch, students went back to their classes and practiced on the state test. You and some of your class-mates have decided it is time to ask to have the 30-minute free playtime reinstated.

Brainstorm ideas on sticky notes or Padlet, and then follow this plan to practice the structural frame of leadership.

1. From all the ideas, determine one goal:

   _____

   _____

   _____

2. List all of details that will be needed to bring your case to the principal.

   _____

   _____

   _____

   _____

   _____

3. Try your ideas on your teacher. Ask your teacher to list the pros and cons of your plan.

Pros	Cons

Creating a Solution

Objectives

In this lesson, students will:
♦ create a problem, and
♦ solve the problem using the structural frame.

Guiding Questions

♦ How do leaders using the structural frame solve everyday problems?
♦ How do leaders using the structural frame organize to solve a problem?

Materials

♦ Handout 12: We Have a Problem
♦ Crayons, colored pencils, or other writing utensils for students
♦ Whiteboard, flipchart, or SmartBoard for discussion

Getting Started

This activity provides an opportunity for students to practice using the structural frame with an everyday problem. Solving the problem is secondary to the process of looking at the solution as a leader using the structural frame. The ultimate purpose of the activity is for them to reflect on leadership during the activity. Students may want to follow up with their solution. If so, move forward with it, but it is not the primary goal of this activity.

Activity

1. Prepare students to determine a problem they have at school. For example, students might focus on noise in the cafeteria, bullying on the playground, or not enough recess or P.E. time. Have students brainstorm in small groups, then come together as one group to determine a problem to solve.
2. Tell students that research shows that leaders are significantly more likely to achieve a goal when they:
   ◇ write the goal down,

DOI:10.4324/9781003236122-14

◇ plan specific action steps,

◇ tell someone about the goal and plan, and

◇ report progress regularly.

3. Distribute Handout 12: We Have a Problem for students to complete.
4. **Talk about it:** Afterward, ask students:

◇ Who took on the primary leadership role?

◇ Did the group set goals, or did one person?

◇ Did you divide into teams in your group? If so, who coordinated each team?

Assessment

Give each student an index card for an in-class response or as an exit card assessment. On the index card, ask students to name a goal they set to solve the problem.

HANDOUT 12

We Have a Problem

Directions: Select a problem to solve as a structural leader. Write a short description of the problem in the center of the circles. Fill in the circles to illustrate the process a leader using the structural frame would use to solve the problem.

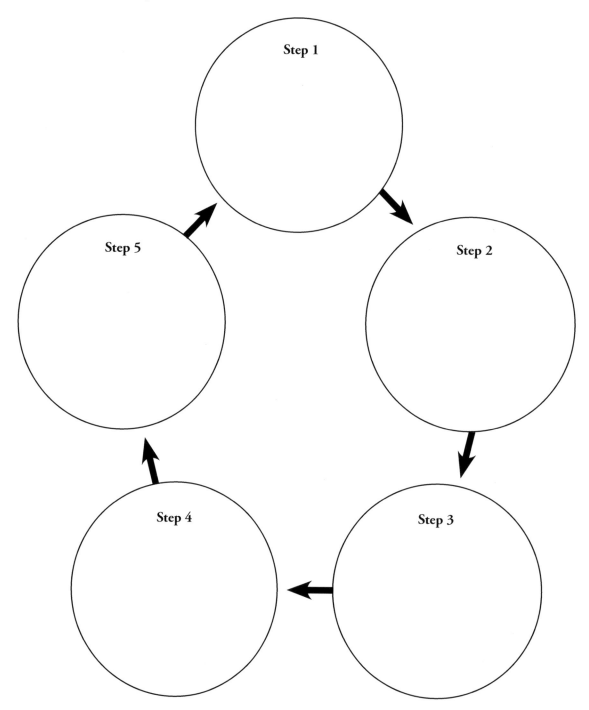

Lesson 13

New Highway

Teacher's Note. The activity will require more time than one class period. It requires research from both primary and secondary sources.

Objectives

In this lesson, students will:
- determine how leaders design goals,
- ensure that details are covered before implementation of a plan, and
- use experimental ideas that lead to problem solutions.

Guiding Questions

- How do goals affect the outcome of a project?
- In what ways are details important for implementation of a plan?
- What is the role of experimentation in problem solving?

Materials

- Handout 13: New Highway
- Crayons, colored pencils, or other writing utensils for students
- Whiteboard, flipchart, or SmartBoard for discussion

Getting Started

Goal setting and attention to detail remain important to a structural leader. In this lesson, students will practice their goal-setting ability as they experiment with probable solutions. They should list all details associated with their goal(s), the plan, and the implementation of the plan. Additional goal-setting activities may be completed before attempting this activity if students have not practiced setting goals. It might also be interesting to see how the students approach goal setting without any instruction.

DOI:10.4324/9781003236122-15

Teacher's Note. If students have limited practice with problem solving before this activity, search electronically for resources to develop problem-solving skills, such as:

- https://www.mindtools.com/pages/article/newTMC_00.htm
- http://www.asa3.org/ASA/education/think/methods.htm

Activity

1. Distribute Handout 13: New Highway and review the instructions with students. Divide students into groups of 3–5. Students will develop a plan for the new highway. Students may build a model if they are interested in doing so.
2. **Talk about it:** At each step in the process, stop and debrief the students about their thinking. For example, after they set their goal for the project, ask them to describe the process they used to determine their goal(s).

Assessment

This is a good activity that can yield multiple assessments (or grades, if needed). Evaluate students' work using a rubric that fits your students' needs (see Lesson 3 for suggested resources). Another assessment would involve evaluating the responses from posting their project on a public forum.

Variation

Instead of posting on a public forum, have students present to the local Board of Trustees or administrators.

Name:_____ Date: _____

New Highway

Directions: Many major highways are overcrowded. You and your team get to create a plan for a new highway. It can be a highway near you, in a major city, in a foreign city, or anywhere that you and your team choose. Your team will approach this activity as a leader using the structural frame would. (A leader using the structural frame sets clear goals, focuses on details and implementation, and experiments with ideas.)

Some things to consider include:

◆ displaced homes and people,
◆ cost of construction,
◆ public input, and
◆ input from experts.

Some websites that may be helpful include the Federal Highway Administration (https://www.fhwa.dot.gov/hep), or your state's highway department (e.g., Texas, http://txdot.gov). You may also want to contact your county/parish's highway department for primary sources.

Submit your project to your state's Department of Transportation blog or post it on another public forum for others to see.

Lesson 14

FrameSpeak

Objectives

In this lesson, students will:

- ◆ determine pros and cons of using the structural frame, and
- ◆ develop an understanding of problem solving that involves all points of view.

Guiding Questions

- ◆ How can a leader using the structural frame involve all parties?
- ◆ What actions define a leader using the structural frame?

Materials

- ◆ Handout 14: A Library Problem
- ◆ Crayons, colored pencils, or other writing utensils for students
- ◆ Whiteboard, flipchart, or SmartBoard for discussion

Getting Ready

This activity solidifies students' understanding of a leader's action using the structural frame in problem solving. This lesson focuses on the pros and cons of leading from the structural frame. Emphasize these statements: *Although people who lead from the structural frame help groups to function well, they may overlook human emotions, political issues, and cultural bonds. They may risk working as rigid micromanagers who limit the strengths that other frames bring to leadership.*

Teacher's Note. The problem that students address in this lesson will be presented again in Lesson 19. The purpose of repeating it is for students to see how the same problem can be used to develop other leadership skills and products. It will add to their repertoire of skills by showing how they may need to solve problems in different ways.

DOI:10.4324/9781003236122-16

Activity

1. Distribute Handout 14: A Library Problem, and discuss the instructions with students. Before beginning, ask students to brainstorm the pros and cons of approaching a problem from the structural frame. Ask what roles will be needed in their team to solve the problem and what others outside the team might need to be included in finding information or solving the problem. Assign teams of three, or let students choose their own teams.

2. **Talk about it:** Afterward, ask students if solving the problem or writing the play was more difficult as a leader using the structural frame. Students should justify their answers with at least three points.

Assessment

Evaluate students' work using a rubric that fits your students' needs (see Lesson 3 for suggested resources).

Variation

Have students present their solution to the campus librarian or the principal.

A Library Problem

Directions: Each of the leader frames exhibit different characteristics. Write a play with two other students that tells how you can solve this problem using the language a leader using the structural frame would use.

Problem: The library does not have enough books for students who can and like to read beyond grade five. How can you solve this problem?

Use these steps to solve the problem:

1. Define the problem.

2. Identify several potential solutions.

3. Evaluate each alternative.

4. Choose a solution.

5. Implement the solution.

6. Evaluate results.

7. Choose a different solution or seek help if results are not satisfactory.

Lessons 15

Timelines

Objectives

In this lesson, students will:
- ◆ solve a problem using the structural frame, and
- ◆ create a timeline with goals and details.

Guiding Questions

- ◆ How do leaders using the structural frame prepare effectively?
- ◆ In what ways does the structural frame facilitate meeting goals along a timeline?

Materials

- ◆ Handout 15: A Problematic Picnic
- ◆ Crayons, colored pencils, or other writing utensils for students
- ◆ Whiteboard, flipchart, or SmartBoard for discussion

Getting Started

Leaders using the structural frame prepare effectively, insist on clear goals, and focus on detail and implementation. Ask students to concentrate on these attributes during this activity, as they learn to solve a problem and create a timeline to illustrate how a leader using the structural frame could work with a large group with a broad set of opinions.

Activity

1. Discuss timelines. Let students research timelines and determine the one they want to use with this lesson's activity. Timelines come in many forms. Let students select the ones that are most meaningful to them. Examples can be found at SmartDraw (https://www.smartdraw.com/organizational-chart/examples) and SIMILE Widgets (http://www.simile-widgets.org/timeline).
2. Distribute Handout 15: A Problematic Picnic and discuss the instructions with students. Divide students into groups of 3–4 to complete the activity.

DOI:10.4324/9781003236122-17

3. **Talk about it:** Debrief the process of problem solving with the students. Ask them to talk about how they created their timeline.

Assessment

Assess how the students participated within their groups. Assess their ability to create a timeline by having them explain their problem-solving process by beginning with their goal and explaining each step they took to reach the goal.

Variation

Instead of creating a timeline for implementation of the solution, have students complete a form that lists pros and cons of their solution.

HANDOUT 15

A Problematic Picnic

Directions: Leaders using each of the frames approach problem solving differently. With your group, think about the following problem, and create a timeline showing the process a leader using the structural frame could use to solve it.

A problem has come up in your school. You are the leader of the group that makes decisions related to student interests. Your group consists of 10 students in the multi-grade class, two from each grade, grades 1–5.

It has come to your attention that a large number of the students in all five grade levels would like to have an all-school picnic prior to spring break. Because of problems in the past, some 10 years ago, this occasion was cancelled and never reinstituted.

You and your group have been asked to create a plan for reinstitution or a presentation to the other students as to why the picnic should remain on hold.

Chapter 2

The Human Resource Frame

❑ Do you like to solve problems with others?

❑ Do you like to share leadership responsibilities?

❑ Do value other students' opinions?

If so, you may prefer to lead from a human resource frame.

The human resource frame focuses on people within the organization. Individuals have needs, feelings, prejudices, skills, and limitations that a leader must consider as he or she guides them in their particular roles. Although the goal of achieving success and completion remains essential to the organization, a leader using the human resource frame cares about the employees or group members and wants them to feel as if they contribute positively to the group. Servant leadership sits at the center of the human resource frame. The metaphor of families (Bolman & Deal, 2014) clarifies the frame as one that supports all team members to function well. Individuals who lead from the human resource frame consistently consider principles focused on the people within the organization. They

♦ communicate a strong belief in people,
♦ develop a philosophy and practices to put their belief in action,
♦ are visible and accessible, and
♦ empower others (p. 49).

When the human resource frame is used, the organization provides an environment that supports group members and allows them to use their gifts and abilities.

DOI:10.4324/9781003236122-18

The leader instills the values of trust, transparency, and democracy. He or she hires the right people and provides professional learning opportunities to strengthen the team. Collaboration and empowerment support the decision-making process. Some simple questions that drive the decision-making process for leaders using a human resource frame (Bolman & Deal, 2014) include:

- What philosophy and values will you follow?
- What will you look for in the people you hire?
- How will you keep people once they sign on?
- What will you do to invest in your people?
- How will you empower your people?
- How will you promote diversity? (pp. 59–60)

The human resource frame helps leaders think beyond the rational, structural thinking in order to motivate team members. They build organizations that benefit from the strengths of the employees. However, these leaders may leave subordinates confused and frustrated because of a lack of clear direction. They must use the skills of advocacy and structure found in other frames to create a cohesive, well-functioning organization.

Lesson 16

Card Stacking

Objectives

In this lesson, students will:
- collaborate to solve a problem, and
- communicate nonverbally to complete a task.

Guiding Questions

- Why is it important for leaders to communicate using the human resource frame when working in a group?
- How do leaders using the human resource frame collaborate with others to solve problems?

Materials

- Handout 16: Card Stacking
- Several packs of index cards (approximately 1,000 cards)

Getting Started

The human resource frame focuses on human needs and abilities to facilitate organizational tasks. This activity helps students understand the importance of communication in teamwork. They learn to rely on persons who exhibit the particular knowledge and skills to guide the group as needed.

Activity

1. Divide students into groups of 5–6 and provide large stacks of index cards to each group. Distribute Handout 16: Card Stacking, and review the instructions.
2. Have groups complete the first part of activity without talking or writing notes to each other.
3. **Talk about it:** Have students debrief about communication and teamwork using the human resource frame. Ask:
   ◇ What made the task difficult?

◇ Did you develop some strategies to build the structure even though you could not talk?

◇ Did someone emerge as a leader in the group? What did he or she do that made him or her the leader?

◇ Did everyone stay involved with the group?

◇ Did you feel like you were competing with the other groups? Did the guidelines tell you to compete?

◇ Did you borrow ideas from other groups? Did the guidelines limit that?

◇ What helped you work as a team in this activity?

4. Distribute more index cards. Groups should work to connect their group's structure with another group's.

5. **Talk about it:** When each group has successfully met the goal, follow up with a discussion of the differences between the first and second activity. Discuss the use of teamwork and empowerment within the human resource frame. For example, you could ask students if one way helped them practice the human resource frame better than the other and why or why not.

Assessment

Ask students to individually complete this 3-2-1 assessment on a large index card or on paper:

◆ List three problems your group encountered during the activity.

◆ Write two solutions your group used to deal with these problems.

◆ Explain one way that leaders using the human resource frame empower group members.

Card Stacking

Part I

Directions: Work in small groups using the index cards to build the largest three-dimensional structure possible within 10 minutes.

1. One problem: You cannot talk or write notes to team members as you work.

2. Do not talk or write notes to each other prior to beginning this task or during the task. No sounds whatsoever. No drawing or illustrating either.

3. Work in the area provided for you for 10 minutes.

4. Do not use anything to support your building other than the index cards (e.g., chairs, tables, clips, notebooks, etc.).

5. If the structure falls, you must start over.

Part II

Now, you must work together to connect your group's structure to another group's structure. The connection must be three-dimensional as well. You must follow the same guidelines of not talking, drawing, or using something for support. You have 10 minutes to complete this task.

Lesson 17

Bookmarking

Objectives

In this lesson, students will:
- ◆ identify keywords and phrases related to the human resource frame, and
- ◆ use the keywords and phrases as a reference for the human resource frame.

Guiding Questions

- ◆ Who is a leader who works from a human resource frame?
- ◆ What are some actions of a leader who uses a human resource frame?

Materials

- ◆ Handout 17: Bookmarking the Human Resource Frame
- ◆ Crayons, colored pencils, or other writing utensils for students
- ◆ Whiteboard, flipchart, or SmartBoard for discussion

Getting Started

This activity serves to familiarize students with terms related to the human resource frame.

Activity

1. Introduce students to the human resource frame. Read aloud the description on pp. 55–56.
2. Distribute Handout 17: Bookmarking the Human Resource Frame. Students will create bookmarks to remind them of the main characteristics of the human resource frame. They may write or draw their ideas.
3. **Talk about it:** Have students read the words or phrases on their bookmarks aloud or discuss any drawings they created. Listeners should check off all of the words they hear that are the same as theirs.

Assessment

No grades should be assigned.

Variation

Students could list their words on a collective poster and create their sentences as a group.

DOI:10.4324/9781003236122-20

Name:_____ Date: _____

Bookmarking the Human Resource Frame

Directions: Create a bookmark to remind you of the main characteristics of the frame a human resource leader uses. You may write or draw your ideas. Then, cut out your bookmark so you can keep it for reference.

Lesson 18

Tic-Tac-Toe

Objectives

In this lesson, students will:

- solve a problem from the perspective of leaders using the human resource frame, and
- respond to unexpected problems.

Guiding Questions

- How do leaders using the human resource frame guide problem solving?
- How do leaders using the human resource frame respond to unexpected problems?

Materials

- Handout 18: School Assembly Disaster
- Crayons, colored pencils, or other writing utensils for students
- Whiteboard, flipchart, or SmartBoard for discussion

Getting Started

The human resource frame addresses those leaders who look to empower the group. This type of leader wants everyone in the group to participate in decision making and goal attainment. This leader supports the group by sharing information, being available for discussions, and encouraging each person's input. This lesson includes a problem-solving activity that requires all students to participate in finding a solution.

Activity

1. Distribute Handout 18: School Assembly Disaster. (*Note*. The tic-tac-toe will require more time than one class period.) Say to students: *Work in groups of no more than three to solve the problem in the scenario. After coming up with a solution, complete the tic-tac-toe, and be ready to present one of your products.*
2. Have students display one of their products and take a gallery walk.

DOI:10.4324/9781003236122-21

3. **Talk about it:** Afterward, ask students if they have any new ideas about leaders and leadership. Discuss their thoughts.

Assessment

Evaluate students' work using a rubric that fits your students' needs (see Lesson 3 for suggested resources). Students can evaluate each other using the rubric to determine if they understand the human resource frame.

HANDOUT 18

School Assembly Disaster

Directions: Read the following problem scenario. Then, complete the tic-tac-toe by selecting three activities that make a row across, down, or diagonally in order to solve the problem. Be ready to share one of your products with the class.

Once a month, our school has an assembly program. Each grade takes a turn securing a program or performing it. This month, grades 3 and 4 have decided to work together for a variety show.

All of the acts have been decided, and it is 30 minutes before showtime. When the two grades head to the school's auditorium, they discover that all of the props are missing and the main act singers are not at school. They have only a short time to find the props and substitute for the main act.

Create a cartoon showing the steps you took to solve the problem.	Write a poem about how you solved the problem from the human resource frame.	Draw a stick picture of a person. Start at the legs and move up the body to the head, labeling the parts of the body with the parts of your problem-solving plan. Label all parts of the plan.
Make a list of priorities for solving the problem.	Make a file of important facts to remember in problem solving as a leader using the human resource frame.	Create a graphic organizer showing how you solved the problem.
Design a plan for school assembly programs that can avoid this situation in the future.	Create a foldable book illustrating your assembly program.	Design a bookmark with important facts about problem solving.

Lesson 19

FrameSpeak

Objectives

In this lesson, students will:
- ◆ determine what an agenda contains, and
- ◆ explore how leaders using the human resource frame would create an agenda.

Guiding Questions

- ◆ In what ways does the human resource frame guide a leader?
- ◆ What are some actions in guiding a group that a leader using the human resource frame would show?

Materials

- ◆ Handout 19: A Library Problem
- ◆ Crayons, colored pencils, or other writing utensils for students
- ◆ Whiteboard, flipchart, or SmartBoard for discussion

Getting Started

Leaders using the human resource frame focus on people within the organization. Individuals have needs, feelings, prejudices, skills, and limitations that a leader must consider as he or she guides them in their particular roles. Although the goal of achieving success and completion remains essential to the organization, a leader using the human resource frame cares about the employees or group members and wants them to feel as if they contribute positively to the group. This activity leads students' thinking about how to create a meeting using a human resource frame as a guide.

Activity

1. Distribute Handout 19: A Library Problem for students to complete.
2. **Talk about it:** Afterward, ask students to select a partner to complete a think-pair-share with the agenda they each created. Students will think about their agendas, pair to discuss each of their agendas, and share their conclusions with the rest of the class.

DOI:10.4324/9781003236122-22

Assessment

Evaluate students' work using a rubric that fits your students' needs (see Lesson 3 for suggested resources).

Variation

Instead of creating an agenda for a meeting, ask students to solve the issue using another problem-solving method. Suggested resources include:

- https://www.mindtools.com,
- http://asq.org/learn-about-quality/problem-solving/overview/overview.html, or
- http://www.educational-business-articles.com/5-step-problem-solving.

A Library Problem

Directions: The library doesn't have enough books for students who can and like to read beyond grade 5. How can you solve this problem? Create an agenda for a meeting of the elementary librarian, the middle school librarian, and you that a leader using the human resource frame would develop.

Lesson 20

Rules

Objectives

In this lesson, students will:
- define rules that guide the human resource frame, and
- compare and contrast the human resource frame with the structural frame.

Guiding Questions

- What rules guide the human resource frame?
- In what ways do rules guide each leadership frame?

Materials

- Handout 20: Comparing Frames
- Crayons, colored pencils, or other writing utensils for students
- Whiteboard, flipchart, or SmartBoard for discussion

Getting Started

Rules are presented not as hard-and-fast regulations but as concrete expressions of the frames. (Refer to Dr. Sandra Kaplan's work with Depth and Complexity for further understanding of *rules* as the term is used here: http://www.byrdseed.com/introducing-depth-and-complexity.) In this lesson, students make connections between the human resource frame and structural frame by looking at rules that define each.

Activity

1. Distribute Handout 20: Comparing Frames for students complete. Students are asked to define a human resource leader by listing three rules that define this frame. They also list three rules for the structural frame as a means of review.
2. **Talk about it:** Afterward, have students discuss the following question: *In what ways do rules guide each leadership frame?* Make sure students support

DOI:10.4324/9781003236122-23

their responses with facts and understanding of the leadership frames they have studied so far.

Assessment

Give students participation grades that include their ability to state facts and relate understanding of the human resource and structural frames.

Variation

Provide three rules each from the human resource and structural frames, and ask students to match the rules with the frame.

HANDOUT 20

Comparing Frames

Directions: Rules are stated and unstated procedures or protocols. They have a structure and a form. If you were a leader using the human resource frame, what are three rules that would guide you?

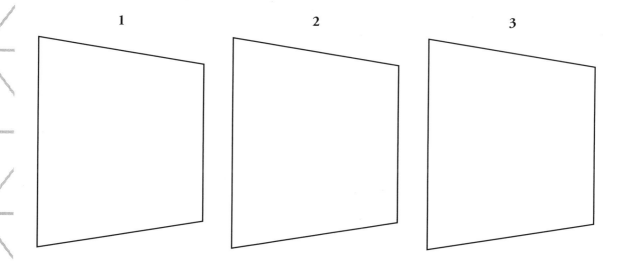

If you were a leader using the structural frame, what are three rules that would guide you?

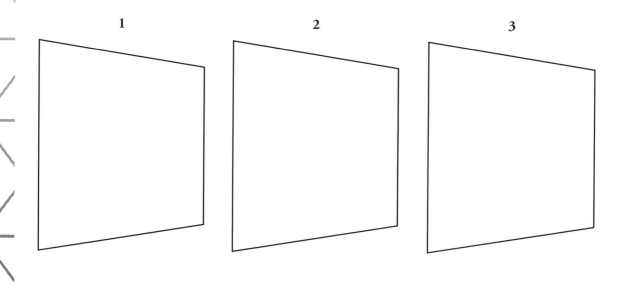

Lesson 21

Timelines

Objectives

In this lesson, students will:
- develop an understanding of using the human resource frame in solving a problem, and
- organize thoughts to create a timeline of events.

Guiding Questions

- How does a leader using the human resource frame organize a group to solve a problem?
- In what ways does a leader using the human resource frame collaborate and empower the group to solve a problem?

Materials

- Handout 21: An Energy Problem
- Crayons, colored pencils, or other writing utensils for students
- Whiteboard, flipchart, or SmartBoard for discussion

Getting Ready

When the human resource frame is used, the organization provides an environment that supports group members and allows them to use their gifts and abilities. The leader instills the values of trust, transparency, and democracy. In this lesson, students will understand how collaboration and empowerment support the decision-making process.

Activity

1. Discuss timelines. Let students research timelines and determine the one they want to use with this lesson's activity. Refer back to Lesson 15 for timeline examples.
2. Distribute Handout 21: An Energy Problem, and discuss the instructions with students. Divide students into groups of 2–4 to complete the activity.

DOI:10.4324/9781003236122-24

3. **Talk about it:** Debrief about the problem-solving process. Ask students to talk about how they created their timeline.

Assessment

Evaluate students' work using a rubric that fits your students' needs (see Lesson 3 for suggested resources).

Variation

Have students solve the problem, then fill in the timeline from the solution back to the beginning.

An Energy Problem

Directions: Leaders using each of the frames approach problem solving differently. With your group, think about the following problem, and create a timeline showing the process a leader using the human resource frame could use to solve it.

The district is considering a new form of energy to supply all district needs. Your school will be the leading campus for the entire school district as it determines its energy sources.

The district's first consideration is wind energy. Your campus will start the process. Create a timeline showing steps with dates to complete the change from the electric company to a wind source company that can supply all of the campuses' electrical needs.

Lesson 22

Trends

Objectives

In this lesson, students will:

◆ recognize trends of leadership in media, and
◆ relate media trends to the human resource frame.

Guiding Questions

◆ What are current trends in leadership?
◆ How do current trends in leadership compare and contrast to the human resource frame?

Materials

◆ Handout 22: KWLT
◆ Crayons, colored pencils, or other writing utensils for students
◆ Whiteboard, flipchart, or SmartBoard for discussion

Getting Started

The human resource frame helps leaders think beyond rational, structural thinking in order to motivate team members. They build organizations that benefit from the strengths of the employees. This activity combines an understanding of trends and the human resource frame. For more information about trends, review trends from Dr. Sandra Kaplan's Elements of Depth and Compelxity at http://www.byrdseed.com/introducing-depth-and-complexity.

Activity

1. Say to students: *Trends are ongoing factors that influence a topic. Using newspapers and any online media, you will look for examples of trends in leadership that exemplify the human resource frame.*
2. Distribute Handout 22: KWLT for students to complete in groups of 2–3. Tell students that KWLT stands for "What I Know" (K), "What I Want to Know" (W), "What I Learned" (L), and "Examples of This Trend" (T).

DOI:10.4324/9781003236122-25

3. **Talk about it:** Afterward, ask students to discuss one trend they found, and ask other students to reply with the following: "This is an example of the human resource frame because . . . "

Assessment

Give students 50% of their grade for finding an example and 50% for being able to identify the human resource frame in other students' examples.

Variation

Ask students to create a bulletin board of their findings that describe structural and human resource frames.

KWLT

Directions: Trends are ongoing factors that influence a topic. Using newspapers and online media, look for examples of trends in leadership that exemplify the human resource frame using KWLT (pronounced "quilt").

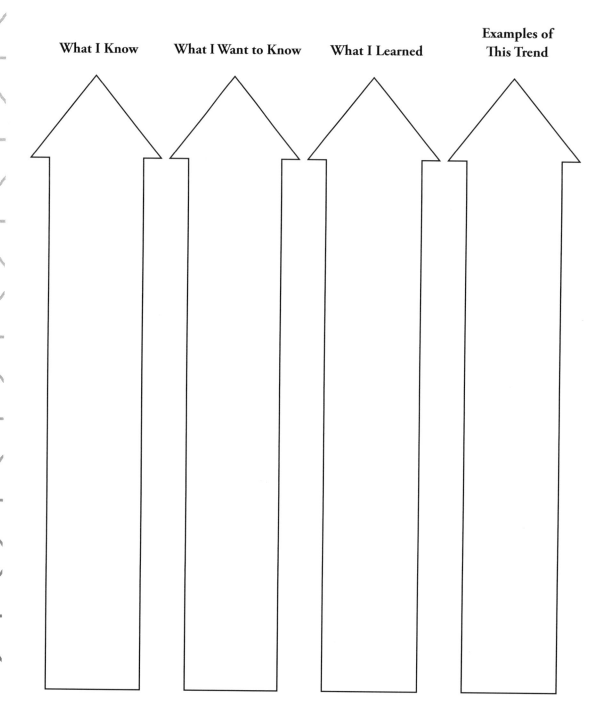

What I Know   **What I Want to Know**   **What I Learned**   **Examples of This Trend**

Lesson 23

We Have a Problem

Objectives

In this lesson, students will:
- create a problem, and
- solve the problem from the human resource frame.

Guiding Questions

- How do leaders using the human resource frame construct a problem?
- What process would leaders using the human resource frame employ to solve a problem?

Materials

- Handout 23: We Have a Problem
- Crayons, colored pencils, or other writing utensils for students
- Whiteboard, flipchart, or SmartBoard for discussion

Getting Started

The human resource frame helps leaders think beyond rational, structural thinking in order to motivate team members. They build organizations that benefit from the strengths of the employees. But these leaders may leave subordinates confused and frustrated because of a lack of clear direction.

Activity

1. Distribute Handout 23: We Have a Problem for students to complete. Students must select a problem to solve that is relevant to them (e.g., too much homework, not enough science experiment time, not enough time to read for fun). Do not judge their choices unless they fall outside ethical boundaries.
2. **Talk about it:** Students must explain to the group why they created their solution to solve their problem.

DOI:10.4324/9781003236122-26

Assessment

Grade the process, not the content. Students must have at least two steps to each part of their process.

Variation

Students could conduct a survey of students from another grade level to determine what problems they have at school. For example, they could survey or interview kindergarten students or students in the grade ahead of them.

We Have a Problem

Directions: Select a problem to solve as a human resource leader would solve it. Write a short description of the problem above the graphic. Fill in the boxes to illustrate the process a leader using the human resource frame would use to solve the problem.

The Problem:

Step 1	Step 2	Step 3
◆	◆	◆
◆	◆	◆
◆	◆	◆

Lesson 24

Show Your Stuff

Objectives

In this lesson, students will:
- describe characteristics of a leader using the human resource frame, and
- develop a definition of the human resource frame.

Guiding Questions

- What does leadership look like in a person using the human resource frame?
- What are some actions of leaders using the human resource frame?

Materials

- Handout 24: Human Resource Graphic
- Crayons, colored pencils, or other writing utensils for students
- Whiteboard, flipchart, or SmartBoard for discussion

Getting Ready

This culminating activity ensures students understand the human resource frame, which focuses on people within an organization. Although the goal of achieving success and completion of goals remains essential to the organization, a leader using the human resource frame cares about the employees or group members and wants them to feel as if they contribute positively to the group.

Activity

1. Distribute Handout 24: Human Resource Graphic. Have students complete this activity individually so that they can reflect on their understanding of the human resource frame and its implications for leadership.
2. Select one part of the graphic for each student to display around the room. If there are more than six students, let students select which part they want to display, making sure all six are covered.
3. **Talk about it:** Have students explain their work.

DOI:10.4324/9781003236122-27

Assessment

Evaluate students' work using a rubric that fits your students' needs (see Lesson 3 for suggested resources).

Variation

Have students take their graphic and create a play, poem, short story, or scenario to express their learning.

Human Resource Graphic

Directions: Complete the graphic using what you know about the human resource frame.

Example.

Define *human resource frame.*

Draw a picture of a leader using the human resource frame.

Human resource frame in one word.

Nonexample.

A person you know who uses the human resource frame.

Chapter 3

The Political Frame

❏   Do you like to negotiate?

❏   Do you think like a politician?

❏   Do you look for people who think about problems the way you do?

If so, you may be a leader who uses the political frame.

The political frame views the world from a position of issues and interest groups. Every group or organization involves individuals and groups with diverse interests and values who compete for scarce resources. Leaders who have strength in the political frame use particular skills to make decisions that meet some of group members' needs but also further the goals of the organization. These leaders must master four key skills: "agenda setting, mapping the political terrain, networking and forming coalitions, and bargaining and negotiating" (Bolman & Deal, 2014, p. 81). The metaphor of the jungle supports the concept of an organization as an arena or contest that needs leaders to advocate, negotiate, and sometimes fight to move the decision-making process forward. In this jungle, coalitions form and special interests emerge that require a leader with political skill. Leaders who use the political frame effectively use several methods. They

♦   clarify what they want and what they can get;

♦   assess the distribution of power and interests;

♦   build linkages to key stakeholders; and

♦   persuade first, negotiate second, and coerce only if necessary (p. 77).

DOI:10.4324/9781003236122-28

When the political frame is used effectively, the leader manages the political dynamics to understand and cope with diverse interests and needs. Although conflict plays a key role in the political frame, the leader negotiates with allies and adversaries to achieve the appropriate agenda for the organization. Some leaders prefer the calm waters of the structural and human resource frames, but at times, they must use the political frame or surround themselves with others who are willing to be the warrior or the peacemaker. Conflict can be a barrier that prevents leaders from achieving their dreams or a powerful lever for change. In order to implement necessary change, members of the organization with diverse views must come on board and take ownership of the change. Four essential questions that help to focus the political frame are:

- Does this situation call for a warrior or peacemaker?
- Who are your allies or opponents?
- What resources do you need to accomplish your goal?
- What strategies will you use to engage your allies or opponents in order to reach success?

Lesson 25

Building Consensus

Objectives

In this lesson, students will:

- build consensus to make a choice, and
- role-play the process of making a group decision.

Guiding Questions

- Why is it important for leaders using the political frame to build consensus in order to make decisions in a group?
- How do leaders using the political frame build a foundation to generate support for a decision?

Materials

- Handout 25.1: T-Shirt Consensus
- Handout 25.2: Group Member Roles (one copy per group; cut into strips and put in an envelope)

Getting Ready

Leaders use the political frame to build coalitions and consensus to move their ideas forward. These leaders must deal with competition, power, and conflict to accomplish their goals. This activity helps students understand the importance of building consensus to make decisions. Following the task, students will consider factors that enhance and limit the decision-making process.

Activity

1. Distribute Handout 25.1: T-Shirt Consensus, and divide students into groups of 10–12. Provide each group with an envelope containing the group member roles (see Handout 25.2).
2. Tell students they will complete a consensus-building activity, playing assigned roles that might sabotage the task. Group members will discuss a decision with a group leader facilitating the process.

DOI:10.4324/9781003236122-29

3. Allow groups to work for 15 minutes. Afterward, ask the groups that have not come to consensus if they need more time. If so, then give them 2 minutes. If they are at a stalemate at the end of that time, they must stop discussion.

4. **Talk about it:** Ask students the following questions:
   ◇ How did your group select the leader? Do you think it was fair?
   ◇ If you were not selected to be the leader, how did you feel?
   ◇ What made it difficult to make a decision about the new T-shirts?
   ◇ How were the descriptions of roles on the slips similar to or different from how people acted in previous groups in which you participated?
   ◇ How did you feel about the group members who were making it difficult to make a decision?
   ◇ How did you feel about the role you selected?
   ◇ How did the leader respond to people who were making it difficult to make a decision?
   ◇ How did he or she help build consensus?

Assessment

Ask students to respond to this question on an exit slip: *How can leaders use the political frame to help groups make decisions?*

T-Shirt Consensus

Directions: You will work in a group today to select the color for new T-shirts for your group. Sometimes groups vote to make a decision. In this activity, you cannot vote because we want the entire group to agree. You must come to consensus as a group.

1. Begin by selecting a leader for your group without taking a vote.

2. The leader will pass the envelope around the group. Each person should select a slip and read it without showing anyone or telling anyone what is on the slip.

3. Place the slips back in the envelope.

4. The leader begins the discussion by saying:

   Our group gets to order new T-shirts. We need to decide on the color of the shirts. Everyone in the group gets to express his or her opinion. We need to discuss this decision and come to consensus. We cannot complete the process until everyone agrees. We have 15 minutes to complete our decision. Let's begin our discussion.

Group Member Roles

Teacher's Note. Cut the roles into strips and put them in an envelope.

You care about other people in the group. Because you want everyone to participate, you try to get each person to talk during the decision-making process. Your favorite color is red.

You are a peacemaker so you do not like people to disagree or argue. When group members disagree, you suggest a new color, hoping they will agree. You do not have a particular color preference.

You like to talk and share your opinion during the decision-making process. You like most colors, but you hate the color red.

You do not really have an opinion about the color of T-shirt, so you avoid participating in the decision-making process. You quietly observe the group interactions and speak very little. Even when you are asked directly, you do not give a specific preference of color.

You really wanted to be the leader, but you were not selected. Because you think you could do a better job than the leader, you work to discredit the leader. You interrupt the leader often to share your own ideas. When the leader suggests a color, you suggest a different color.

You prefer to work alone, so this group process is not something you enjoy. You find something wrong with everyone else's ideas. You like green and will stay with this color regardless of others' suggestions.

You like to hear yourself talk—so you ask many questions. You even start talking about other topics that do not involve making a decision about the T-shirt color. You often begin by saying, "That reminds me of . . ." You want the color navy.

Handout 25.2, Continued.

You are a very creative free spirit. You think of yourself as different from the other people in the group. Because you like unusual things, you suggest unique colors like fluorescent pink or lime green.

You want to help the decision-making process, so you ask questions to help move the process forward. You express your opinion, but you try to get others on board with the decisions. You do not have a particular color preference but listen to the group members and logically consider the options.

You are a follower, not a leader. Because you like many colors, you choose to follow others' ideas. Even though you like yellow, you often agree to select another color that someone suggests.

You want to feel included and participate as part of the team. You jump on board when others make suggestions as long as the color is not yellow. If the group comes close to a decision, you step in and try to wrap things up for the leader.

You do not care about the color for the T-shirt, so you agree with anyone who gives an opinion. You joke about the ridiculousness of the group having to make this decision. You kid around with the people sitting next to you, so people in the group do not take you seriously.

The Gist of Political Leadership

Objectives

In this lesson, students will:
- identify keywords and phrases related to the political frame, and
- find keywords and phrases as a reference for the political frame.

Guiding Questions

- Who is a leader who works from a political frame or point of view?
- What are some actions of a leader who works from a political frame or point of view?

Materials

- Handout 26: Bookmarking the Political Frame
- Crayons, colored pencils, or other writing utensils for students
- Whiteboard, flipchart, or SmartBoard for discussion

Getting Ready

This activity helps to familiarize students with the terms related to the political frame.

Activity

1. Introduce students to the political frame. Read aloud the description on pp. 83–84.
2. Distribute Handout 26: Bookmarking the Political Frame. Students will create bookmarks to remind them of the main characteristics of the political frame. They may write or draw their ideas.
3. **Talk about it:** Have students read the words or phrases on their bookmarks aloud or discuss any drawings they created. Listeners should check off all of the words they hear that are the same as theirs.

DOI:10.4324/9781003236122-30

Assessment

No grades should be assigned.

Variation

Students could list their words on a collective poster and create their sentences as a group.

Bookmarking the Political Frame

Directions: Create a bookmark to remind you of the main characteristics of the frame a political leader uses. You may write or draw your ideas. Then, cut out your bookmark so you can keep it for reference.

Lesson 27

Graphic Leaders

Objectives

In this lesson, students will:
- ◆ cite characteristics of leaders using the political frame, and
- ◆ name five people who exhibit these characteristics and tell about those people.

Guiding Questions

- ◆ How can you recognize someone using the political frame in problem solving?
- ◆ Who are some leaders who use the political frame for problem solving?

Materials

- ◆ Handout 27: Two Hands
- ◆ Crayons, colored pencils, or other writing utensils for students
- ◆ Whiteboard, flipchart, or SmartBoard for discussion

Getting Ready

Leaders using the political frame serve as advocates. They know how to set an agenda, understand the politics of the group as a whole, network and build coalitions, and practice their bargaining and negotiating skills. This lesson will familiarize students with how a political leader can determine informal channels of communication, find the persons of influence, find people who will work to achieve the goal, and foresee issues that arise from those who do not share the vision.

Activity

1. Introduce the study of the structural frame by reviewing characteristics of a leader using the political frame (pp. 27–28).
2. Distribute Handout 27: Two Hands for students to complete.
3. **Talk about it:** Have students present their leaders who use the political frame and explain why they selected one of the leaders. Students should share why, how, and when the person uses the political frame.

DOI:10.4324/9781003236122-31

Assessment

Evaluate students' work using a rubric that fits your students' needs (see Lesson 3 for suggested resources).

Variation

Refer back to Lesson 8 and ask students to compare and contrast their choices.

Two Hands

Directions: Use the hand graphic organizers to respond to the following prompts.

First Hand: List five attributes of a leader using the political frame. Write the characteristic that is most important to you in the palm of the hand.

Handout 27, Continued.

Second Hand: List five people who lead using a political frame. In the palm, write why you have chosen one of the five.

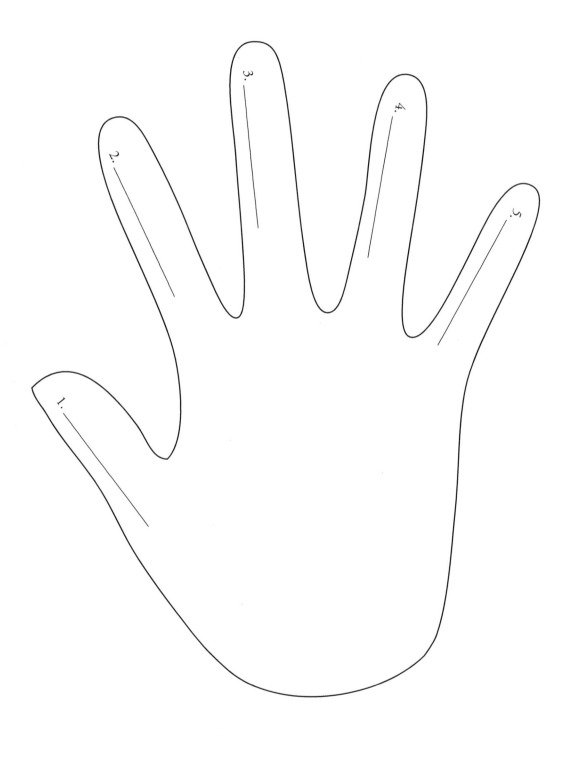

Lesson 28

Spy Game

Teacher's Note. The activity will require more time than one class period. It also requires specialized materials.

Objectives

In this lesson, students will:
- use the political frame in problem creation and problem solving, and
- create scenarios and videos of their work with the "spy mission."

Guiding Questions

- In what ways would one who uses the political frame determine a target mission?
- In what ways would one who uses the political frame solve a problem through a spy mission?

Materials

- Video equipment
- Student computer and Internet access
- Various props
- Crayons, colored pencils, or other writing utensils for students
- Whiteboard, flipchart, or SmartBoard for planning

Getting Ready

Leaders use the political frame to build coalitions and consensus to move their ideas forward. These leaders must deal with competition, power, and conflict to accomplish their goals. This lesson provides an opportunity for students to practice their skills using the political frame to develop skills with problem creation and problem solution.

DOI:10.4324/9781003236122-32

Activity

1. Tell students that they are on a spy mission. Their target is unknown. Students will work in groups of 3–4 to determine a target (problem creation), a mission (problem solving), disguises, and subterfuges. For example, students could work on a problem particular to their town/city or an issue with their sibling(s). They should decide how to communicate among the group, who are allies and who are opponents, what roles each group member will play, and how to know that the target has been reached successfully (a solution).

2. Once they have developed their plan, have groups create video narratives of their missions. The videos will show how they used the political frame to create the mission, determine the group's responsibilities, and solve the mission. Students may use any props they need and access ideas through various sources of information. They will need equipment to create the videos and to share their videos with the class. This activity could be effectively shared with other students, administrators, and/or parents.

3. **Talk about it:** Debrief students about how they determined the target missions, how they chose each of the roles of the group, how they solved the mission, and how they used the political frame in the activity.

Assessment

Students will judge each other's video presentations. You may create a rubric that best evaluates the work of your students.

Lesson 29

FrameSpeak

Objectives

In this lesson, students will:
- know how to use the political frame to communicate their solution to a problem, and
- present their solution to a school administrator.

Guiding Questions

- How do you solve problems using the political frame?
- How do you communicate with a group using the political frame?
- How do you communicate your problem's solution to adults by using the political frame?

Materials

- Handout 29: A Cafeteria Problem
- Props, visual aids, technology
- Crayons, colored pencils, or other writing utensils for students
- Whiteboard, flipchart, or SmartBoard for discussion

Getting Ready

When the political frame is used effectively, the leader manages the political dynamics to understand and cope with diverse interests and needs. Although conflict plays a key role in the political frame, the leader negotiates with allies and adversaries to achieve the appropriate agenda for the organization. This activity offers students an occasion to work with a familiar problem and solve it through the political frame. (*Note.* If a more pressing problem emerges for your students, you may change the problem. The process will remain the same.)

Activity

1. Distribute Handout 29: A Cafeteria Problem for students to complete. As students work on the solution, they may create visuals or other props. Students

DOI:10.4324/9781003236122-33

should practice their dialogue, anticipate questioning by the principal, and use their skill with the political frame to prepare for a conversation.

2. **Talk about it:** Ask students to reflect on their dialogue by thinking about how they structured it for an adult audience:

   ◇ How was it alike and different from presenting to their peers?

   ◇ How did knowledge of the political frame help in creating their solution?

   ◇ How did it help in the dialogue with the principal?

Assessment

Ask the principal to provide an evaluation of the presentation(s). Use his or her comments for a discussion with students about how to use critiques of their work. If a grade is necessary, evaluate students' work using a rubric that fits your students' needs (see Lesson 3 for suggested resources).

Variation

Students may write their problem and solution as an editorial for the local newspaper or present their work to the local Board of Trustees.

A Cafeteria Problem

Directions: Leaders using each of the frames exhibit different characteristics. Create a dialogue between you and the principal that tells how you can solve this problem using the political frame.

> The cafeteria is crowded and noisy during your lunchtime. Every table is filled, and when the room gets too noisy, you cannot hear what your friends are saying. Sometimes the teachers get tired of all the noise, so they will not let anyone speak. Lunch is the only time you can really visit with friends, so everyone is upset.

Lesson 30

More FrameSpeak

Objectives

In this lesson, students will:

♦ use the political frame to explain their solution to a community problem, and

♦ create a myth that incorporates the problem and solution from a political frame.

Guiding Questions

♦ Does your issue call for a warrior or peacemaker?

♦ Who are allies or opponents?

♦ What part do allies or opponents play in the success of the solution?

Materials

♦ Props, visual aids, technology

♦ Crayons, colored pencils, or other writing utensils for students

♦ Whiteboard, flipchart, or SmartBoard for discussion

Getting Ready

This activity offers an opportunity for students to create a problem and solution using their creativity with writing and acting out myths. Use myths students already know (e.g., Paul Bunyan, Legend of the Bluebonnet). As the students work on the problem solution, they may create visuals or other props. Planet Ozkids (http://www.planetozkids.com/oban/legends.htm) and Education World (http://www.education-world.com/a_lesson/lesson/lesson279.shmtl) are good resources for this activity.

Activity

1. Using a community problem of their choosing, ask students to write one myth to explain how the issue became a problem. Their myths must include:

◇ local characters as animals or superheroes,

◇ pros and cons of the issue,

◇ allies and adversaries that created the problem,

DOI:10.4324/9781003236122-34

◇ the role of warriors and peacemakers, and

◇ strategies used to engage your allies or opponents in order to reach success.

2. Afterward, students may present their myths in any product they choose. As students prepare, remind them of the role the political frame plays in developing their myth. Use the product list in Lesson 5.

3. **Talk about it:** Ask students:

◇ What resources were needed to accomplish the solution?

◇ What strategies did you use to develop your myth?

Assessment

Evaluate students' work using a rubric that fits your students' needs (see Lesson 3 for suggested resources).

Variation

Students may offer their product to another grade level or compile all of their myths into a book for the library or an eBook available to all grade levels.

Lesson 31

Ping-Pong Pyramid

Objectives

In this lesson, students will:
- create the concept of a pyramid using strategies of the political frame, and
- build a pyramid with the five sets of ping-pong balls.

Guiding Questions

- How does a group using the political frame create a conceptual plan?
- What roles are required to develop a plan and to construct the ping-pong pyramid?

Materials

- Ping-pong balls (one set of 20 per group glued into the five configurations show in Figure 1)
- Chart paper
- Whiteboard, flipchart, or SmartBoard for discussion
- Crayons, colored pencils, or other writing utensils for students

Getting Ready

When the political frame is used effectively, the leader manages the political dynamics to understand and cope with diverse ideas. Although conflict plays a key role in the political frame, the leader negotiates with allies and adversaries to achieve the appropriate ideas for a solution to a current problem. This activity offers an opportunity for students to think conceptually and creatively using the political frame without assigning specific roles.

DOI:10.4324/9781003236122-35

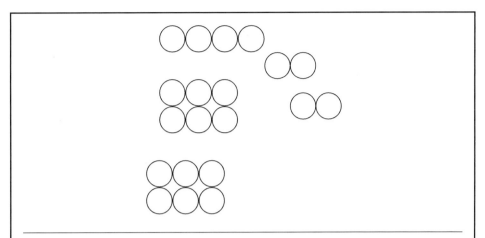

Figure 1. Ping-pong ball configurations. From *Quicksilver: Adventure Games, Initiative Problems, Trust Activities and a Guide to Effective Leadership* (pp. 181–182), by K. Rohnke and S. Butler, 1995, Beverly, MA: Project Adventure. Copyright 1995 by Project Adventure. Reprinted with permission.

Activity[1]

1. Divide students into groups of no more than three. Each group will receive a set of ping-pong balls. Tell students: *Using the five configurations of ping-pong balls, create a pyramid. You may not touch the sets until you have created a plan to make the pyramid. You must list the steps you will use on the chart paper before you attempt building the actual pyramid. As you plan, consider the political frame. You will use the strategies of a political leader to create your solution.*

2. **Talk about it:** For reflection, ask students:
   ◇ Who became the leader?
   ◇ How was the leader decided?
   ◇ How were conflicts handled?

Assessment

Steps listed for building the pyramid may serve as the basis for evaluation. Success with the pyramid may also provide an assessment.

Variation

Have students suggest other objects to use for building a pyramid. Another option is to have them suggest other structures to build using the same process.

---

1   *Note.* This activity is adapted from *Quicksilver: Adventure Games, Initiative Problems, Trust Activities and a Guide to Effective Leadership* (pp. 181–182), by K. Rohnke and S. Butler, 1995, Beverly, MA: Project Adventure. Copyright 1995 by Project Adventure. Adapted with permission.

Lesson 32

Questions and Interviews

Objectives

In this lesson, students will:
- prepare questions for the interview of a local leader, and
- interview a local leader.

Guiding Questions

- What role do good questions play in the interview of a leader?
- How do questions determine information about a leader?

Materials

- Handout 32: Interviewing a Leader
- Interview resources:
  - ◇ "How to Create Structured Interview Questions" (available at http://smallbusiness.chron.com/create-structured-interview-questions-19099.html)
  - ◇ "Lesson 2.2: Interviewing: The Art of Asking Questions" (available at https://studentreportinglabs.org/resource/lesson-22-interviewingthe-art-asking-questions)
  - ◇ "Beyond Question: Learning the Art of the Interview" (available at https://learning.blogs.nytimes.com/2010/09/20/beyond-question-learning-the-art-of-the-interview)

- List of local leaders
- Video and audio equipment
- Whiteboard, flipchart, or SmartBoard for brainstorming questions
- Crayons, colored pencils, or other writing utensils for students

Getting Ready

This activity is about asking good questions, learning how to interview, and applying questions to the political frame. The activity encompasses three sections and will require more class time than most activities.

DOI:10.4324/9781003236122-36

Activity

1. Review characteristics of the political frame.
2. Distribute Handout 32: Interviewing a Leader, and review the instructions.
3. Help students develop questions that will elicit answers relative to a leader who uses the political frame. Students may interview a local civic leader, a school official, or a state senator or representative.
4. Students must practice interviewing before they actually interview their leader. Have students practice with each other and/or video their practice so that they can see and hear themselves as they sound to others. (See Materials list for a list of resources about conducting interviews.) Teachers may want to enlist the help of the principal or speech teacher from the high school to help evaluate students' practice interviews.
5. **Talk about it**: At this point in students' learning, they should feel confident in talking about the political, human resource, and structural frames. Ask the students to identify the work their leader does and how that work relates to the political and human resource frames, if applicable. Also, have students reflect on whether they noticed that the leaders used only one frame or more than one and how that relates to what they do.

Assessment

This activity provides an opportunity to evaluate each step of the interview process. You can assess students' questions, their interview techniques, the interview, their evaluation of the interview, and their reflection on the leader interviewed. Evaluate students' work using a rubric that fits your students' needs (see Lesson 3 for suggested resources).

Variation

Students may interview in pairs.

Interviewing a Leader

Directions: You are doing a television interview (without the TV cameras).

1. Find a local leader you want to interview.

2. Develop questions to ask a local leader about how the person leads others. Your questions should be designed to find out if the leader uses any of the actions from the political frame. Your teacher will help you learn about how to create good questions.

3. After you have your questions ready, learn about how to interview.

4. Practice interviewing with a partner. You may video your practice so that you hear how your questions sound and see how you look when asking the questions.

5. You are ready for your interview. Call your selected leader to set a time and place for the interview. Plan how you will record the answers. If you record using a video or audio recorder, make sure that you have the permission of the leader to record and the equipment works. If you plan to write your answers, take someone with you to write. You should be focused on the leader and asking the question.

6. After the interview, evaluate the answers to know how or if the leader uses the political frame. You may also want to identify other frames that the leader may use.

Complete this form after the interview:

My Leader: _____

Date/Time of Interview: _____

Examples of Leadership With a Political Frame:

Other Frames I Observed:

Lesson 33

Blogging

Objectives

In this lesson, students will:
- create a blog post about the political frame, and
- describe a leader using the political frame in their blog post.

Guiding Questions

- What is a blog?
- How can you connect with other students studying leadership?

Materials

- Student computer and Internet access
- Kidblog (available at https://kidblog.org)

Getting Ready

This activity guides students to synthesize their learning about the political frame by writing a blog. It provides students with a venue to communicate their learning to students of similar age and interests. This writing experience also provides an opportunity to reinforce rules of plagiarism.

Activity

1. Introduce students to Kidblog, a safe blogging platform for students.

Teacher's Note. If your school district will not allow Kidblog, work with the computer specialist to create an in-house version.

2. Once students have mastered navigating Kidblog, ask them to think about all that they have learned about the political frame. They should write a short blog post about the political frame *in their own words*. In their blog posts, they should write about:
   ◇ characteristics of leaders who use the political frame,
   ◇ the person they interviewed and what they learned in Lesson 32,
   ◇ words that other students will understand when they describe a leader who uses the political frame, and
   ◇ anything else they think will help other students understand the political frame.

3. Tell students that they should also include questions for readers so that they receive responses. The shorter their blog posts are, the better; however, blog posts should still be informative.

4. Have students share responses to their blog post with the class.

5. **Talk about it:** Give students an opportunity to respond with what they learned from the information shared by other students on Kidblog.

Assessment

The number of responses to their blog may serve as a measure of their success. You can also evaluate their syntheses of the new knowledge about leaders using the political frame.

Variation

If technology is not available for this activity, let students create a news story about their learning and present it as if it were a television news story.

Chapter 4

The Symbolic Frame

❏ Do you often feel passionate about a subject or an issue?

❏ Do you have traditions you like to follow?

❏ Do you like to use creative thinking to solve a problem?

If so, you may prefer to lead from the symbolic frame.

The symbolic frame views organizations as cultural environments and leads through rituals, ceremonies, stories, heroes, and myths. Rather than using a rational, structured or person-centered approach, symbolic leaders cast the vision and call others to action through inspiration. The symbolic frame brings meaning and purpose to a group and forms a culture that includes shared patterns that define a "certain way of doing things." The metaphors of tribes, temples, and carnivals call for symbolic leaders to serve as magicians, prophets, or poets (Bolman & Deal, 2014). Just as a tribe looks to their leader for guidance, organizations follow a symbolic leader who is deeply rooted in faith and passions. They catch the passions and follow the dreams of the leader. Leaders using the symbolic frame follow a consistent set of scripts and rituals and share the following characteristics. They:

- ◆ lead by example,
- ◆ use symbols to unite and inspire others,
- ◆ interpret experience,
- ◆ develop and communicate a hopeful vision,
- ◆ tell stories,
- ◆ convene rituals and ceremonies, and
- ◆ respect and use history (p. 106).

DOI:10.4324/9781003236122-38

When symbolic leadership is in place, organizations or groups form meaningful cultures supported by the groups' history and traditions. Rather than plodding through strategic thinking and conflict resolution, the members of the organization are inspired by the hopes and dreams of the leader who addresses the challenges of the present and incorporates the values of the followers. Symbolic leaders recognize and build the spirit needed at the core of any group that is essential to finding meaning and purpose. Four simple questions focus the symbolic frame:

- What specialized language reflects and shapes the group's culture?
- What stories and traditions guide the behavior of the group?
- What rituals and ceremonies reinforce the purpose and hope of the group?
- What informal cultural players reinforce and interpret the vision of the leader?

Organizations need the other three frames to function, but the symbolic frame creates a community and culture shaped by common purpose and values. This frame brings energy and significance to their work: "Peak performance emerges as a team discovers its soul" (Bolman & Deal, 2014, p. 128).

Lesson 34

Making Meaning

Objectives

In this lesson, students will:
- ◆ create meaning by sharing stories of leaders, and
- ◆ call others to action related to issues of interest.

Guiding Questions

- ◆ Why is it important for leaders to create meaning for group members using the symbolic frame?
- ◆ How do leaders using the symbolic frame inspire others to follow their plan and move forward with their ideas?

Materials

- ◆ Handout 34: My Leadership Handprint
- ◆ Construction paper cut in the shape of hands (one per group)

Getting Ready

The symbolic frame creates a vision for an organization or group. Leaders use this frame to bring meaning to a process or initiative. These leaders call people to action to help the organization accomplish goals. This activity helps students reflect on leaders who have brought meaning to their lives and the steps that will call others to action.

Activity

1. Begin the activity by sharing the story of a person who served as a role model or inspired you. With the class, discuss the impact people make in students' lives.
2. Distribute Handout 34: My Leadership Handprint for students to complete, remembering those who inspired them.
3. Afterward, divide students into groups of 3–4 and distribute construction paper handprints. Say to students: *Share the statements you wrote on your handprint with your group. Then, together, brainstorm several issues that are*

DOI:10.4324/9781003236122-39

important to you. Select the one that you think the other students in the class will care about as well. Write the selected issue on a construction paper handprint. Next, consider several statements that will call other students to action related to the issue you selected. Write those statements on the your handprint. Display your group's handprint, and be prepared to share these "call to action" statements with the class in an inspirational way.

4. **Talk about it:** Ask students:

  ◇ What makes a person's influence most memorable?

  ◇ Using the symbolic frame, how does a leader cast a vision for an organization?

  ◇ When you care about an issue, how can you convince others to follow your lead?

  ◇ When new leaders join an organization, how can they get followers to support new initiatives?

  ◇ How does providing meaning and purpose drive an organization?

5. Debrief about how the symbolic frame can help organizations to share a task and mission.

Assessment

Have students write a persuasive essay, calling people to action about a critical issue of interest to them. They can use the issue and steps they created in the activity.

My Leadership Handprint

Directions: In the space below, draw an outline of your hand. Consider role models or inspirations in your life:

1. Label your thumb with a person you admire and why.
2. Label your pointer finger with the name of someone from whom you have learned a lot.
3. Label your middle finger with someone your age who you think is a good leader.
4. Label your ring finger with words you might use to describe someone you think is a role model.
5. Label your pinkie finger with the words you want people to use when describing you as a leader.

Lesson 35

The Gist of Symbolic Leadership

Objectives

In this lesson, students will:
- identify keywords and phrases related to leaders using the symbolic frame, and
- list the keywords and phrases as a reference for the symbolic frame.

Guiding Questions

- Who is a leader who works from a symbolic frame?
- What are some actions of a leader who works from a symbolic frame?

Materials

- Handout 35: Bookmarking the Symbolic Frame
- Crayons, colored pencils, or other writing utensils for students
- Whiteboard, flipchart, or SmartBoard for discussion

Getting Ready

This activity serves to familiarize students with terms related to the symbolic frame.

Activity

1. Introduce students to the symbolic frame. Read aloud the description on pp. 111–112.
2. Distribute Handout 35: Bookmarking the Symbolic Frame. Students will create bookmarks to remind them of the main characteristics of the symbolic frame. They may write or draw their ideas.
3. **Talk about it:** Have students read the words or phrases on their bookmarks aloud or discuss any drawings they created. Listeners should check off words they hear that are the same as theirs.

DOI:10.4324/9781003236122-40

Assessment

No grades should be assigned.

Variation

Students could list their words on a collective poster and create their sentences as a group.

Bookmarking the Symbolic Frame

Directions: Create a bookmark to remind you of the main characteristics of the frame a symbolic leader uses. You may write or draw your ideas. Then, cut out your bookmark so you can keep it for reference.

Lesson 36

Technology and the Symbolic Frame

Objectives

In this lesson, students will:
- use the symbolic frame to influence others, and
- use the symbolic frame along with graphic technology.

Guiding Questions

- In what ways can technology help you as one who uses the symbolic frame in leadership?
- In what ways do graphics enhance communication with the symbolic frame?

Materials

- Handout 36: A Donation Problem
- Student computer and Internet access
- PowToon (available at https://www.powtoon.com/edu-home)
- Crayons, colored pencils, or other writing utensils for students
- Whiteboard, flipchart, or SmartBoard for discussion

Getting Ready

In this lesson, students will practice their skills of persuasion through the symbolic frame and learn how to use technology to present their ideas.

Activity

1. Introduce students to PowToon, an easy-to-use animation software platform. Students will learn how to use PowToon to communicate their ideas by developing a persuasive presentation based on the scenario detailed on Handout 36: A Donation Problem.
2. Tell students they should complete the handout before creating their presentations.

DOI:10.4324/9781003236122-41

3. **Talk about it:** Before students begin their presentations, debrief their ideas and ask students to sketch out their ideas for PowToon.

Assessment

The assessment will rely on two areas: Their planning as a leader using the symbolic frame. A rubric may be applied to this phase and to their PowToon product. Then, the students will assess themselves after their presentation to administrators and/or the school board based on their success or lack of success.

Variation

Students could use other graphics platforms than PowToon if they have already mastered this process. The activity should expose them to a new technology to add to their toolbox of skills.

HANDOUT 36

A Donation Problem

Directions: Use your skills as a symbolic leader to solve the problem described below. Use technology to outline your ideas and create your presentation.

> A carnival owner who graduated from your school has offered to donate a merry-go-round and Ferris wheel to your school's playground. The owner is also a friend of your parents. You think this is a good idea and want to create a team of students to convince the campus and district administration and school board to accept this donation.

1. Our beliefs about the donation:

2. Our goal:

3. Experiences of the planning group that will excite the decision-makers:

4. Our plan:

Lesson 37

Webbing the Symbolic Frame

Objectives

In this lesson, students will:

◆ discuss their thinking about a person who uses the symbolic frame in leadership, and
◆ web their ideas about a person using the symbolic frame.

Guiding Questions

◆ How do you describe a person using the symbolic frame to lead?
◆ Who do you know who is using the symbolic frame to lead?

Materials

◆ Handout 37: Webbing the Symbolic Frame
◆ Crayons, colored pencils, or other writing utensils for students
◆ Whiteboard, flipchart, or SmartBoard for discussion

Getting Ready

This lesson should remind students that leaders using the symbolic frame are those who seek to inspire their organization. They capture attention and interpret the experiences that the group will complete. They set the vision.

Activity

1. Ask students to discuss their understanding of the symbolic frame. Ask how a leader using the symbolic frame is different from their first ideas about a leader.
2. Distribute Handout 37: Webbing the Symbolic Frame for students to complete.
3. **Talk about it:** Ask students to think-pair-share. After sharing their ideas, ask each pair to be ready to give their best ideas to the group.

DOI:10.4324/9781003236122-42

Assessment

Evaluate students' ability to synthesize their ideas.

Variation

Have students choose to use a different style of graphic organizer, either one that they create by hand or on the computer.

HANDOUT 37

Webbing the Symbolic Frame

Directions: Answer the questions by placing answers in the circles.

1. Describe a person who leads using the symbolic frame.
2. In what ways can a person using the symbolic frame contribute as a leader?
3. What are two words that describe a person using the symbolic frame?
4. Name two successful persons using the symbolic frame and their organizations.
5. What makes a person using the symbolic frame different from your first definition of leadership?
6. Look into the future: What person using the symbolic frame will be remembered?

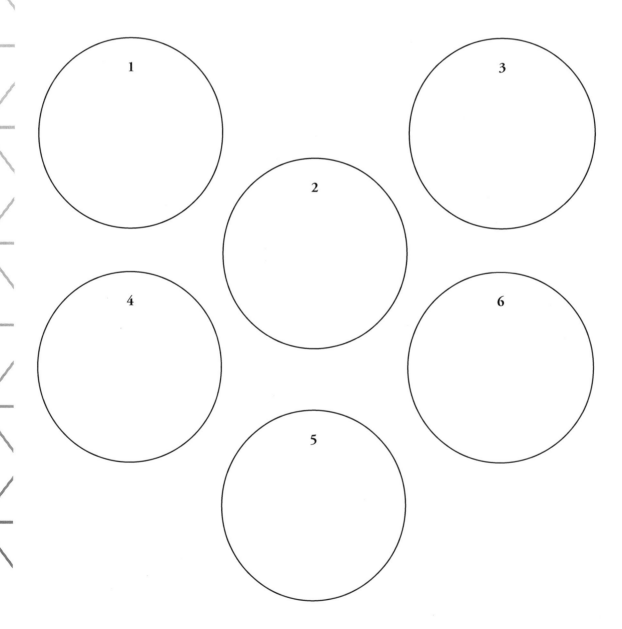

© Taylor & Francis Group • *Leadership for Kids*

Lesson 38

Create-a-Problem

Objectives

In this lesson, students will:
- create a problem to solve using skills of the symbolic frame, and
- create a solution to their problem as a leader using the symbolic frame.

Guiding Question

- In what ways do persons using the symbolic frame determine relevant problems?

Materials

- Handout 38: We Have a Problem
- Crayons, colored pencils, or other writing utensils for students
- Whiteboard, flipchart, or SmartBoard for discussion

Getting Ready

The symbolic frame views organizations as cultural environments and leads through rituals, ceremonies, stories, heroes, and myths. Rather than using a rational, structured or person-centered approach, leaders using a symbolic frame cast the vision and call others to action through inspiration. The symbolic frame brings meaning and purpose to a group and forms a culture that includes shared patterns that define a "certain way of doing things." In this lesson, students will determine a problem in their class, school, district, or town/city and work to solve the problem using the symbolic frame.

Activity

1. Distribute Handout 38: We Have a Problem for students to complete. They may work independently and/or in small groups and be ready to discuss and evaluate their solution(s).
2. **Talk about it:** Have students present their problem and solution for input from other students/groups.

DOI:10.4324/9781003236122-43

Assessment

Assess students' solutions using a Creative Problem Solving evaluation grid:

- ◆ "CPS Model" (available at http://members.optusnet.com.au/charles57/Creative/Brain/cps.htm)
- ◆ "The Osborn-Parnes Model of Creative Problem Solving" (available at https://prezi.com/ae99kapkqx6y/the-osborn-parnes-model-of-creative-problem-solving)
- ◆ Boswell, C., & Carlile, V. (2016). *RTI for the gifted student.* Sundown, TX: Creative Teaching Materials.

Variation

Review the Creative Problem Solving process and have students solve the problem with this process.

We Have a Problem

Directions: Select a problem to solve as a symbolic frame leader would solve it. Write a short description of the problem above the graphic. Fill in the boxes to illustrate the process a leader using the symbolic frame would use to solve the problem.

The Problem:

Step 1	Step 2	Step 3
◆	◆	◆
◆	◆	◆
◆	◆	◆

Lesson 39

Appreciating the Symbolic Frame

Objectives

By the end of this sessions, students will:

- recognize examples and nonexamples of leaders using the symbolic frame, and
- develop a new plan as a leader using the symbolic frame.

Guiding Questions

- In what ways does a leader using the symbolic frame lead by example?
- In what ways does a leader using the symbolic frame communicate a vision?

Materials

- Handout 39: A Bullying Solution
- Crayons, colored pencils, or other writing utensils for students
- Whiteboard, flipchart, or SmartBoard for discussion

Getting Ready

Just as a tribe looks to their leader for guidance, organizations follow a symbolic leader who is deeply rooted in faith and passions. In this activity, students will read the story about two fictional characters and decide if they use the symbolic frame. They must be ready to justify their answers.

Activity

1. Have students think back on what they have learned about the symbolic frame thus far.
2. Distribute Handout 39: A Bullying Solution for students to complete.
3. **Talk about it:** Discuss students' answers to questions on Handout 39.

DOI:10.4324/9781003236122-44

Assessment

By this time, students should know how to articulate what they have learned about the symbolic frame. Evaluate students' work using a rubric that fits your students' needs (see Lesson 3 for suggested resources).

Variation

Students can rewrite the Mary Ellen and Susan story using the symbolic frame if they do not believe Mary Ellen used that frame. Or, they can create a new story that illustrates how a student trying to solve a bullying problem would use the symbolic frame.

A Bullying Solution

Directions: Read the problem scenario below. Then, answer the questions that follow.

Susan has always been a bully. Every fourth grader knows it. So do all the first, second, and third graders. She knows not to mess with the fifth graders. Susan may tell someone that they look poor; she may say that they can't read; or she may trip someone smaller than she is just for fun. And she always seems to get by with it—at least, the teachers and principal can never catch her.

Mary Ellen, a fellow fourth grader, has a plan. Her idea is to get six girls to help her convince Susan that she does not need to be a bully.

She gets a group of fourth-grade girls together during lunch. It may take a while because she doesn't want many people to know about her plan. After 3 days Mary Ellen has shared her idea and has the group of girls ready to move forward with her plan.

Mary Ellen and the girls made a symbol on sticky notes and started placing them on all the girls' book covers, including Susan's. The symbol was a ring of stick figure girls.

No one knew what the symbol meant, but they figured out that Mary Ellen had started the idea. Everyone was asking everyone else what it meant, and Mary Ellen's original group of girls purposefully included Susan in all the speculations.

After about a week, Mary Ellen's group of girls placed sticky notes on book covers that said for all fourth-grade girls to meet on Friday at P.E., their free play day. At the meeting, Mary Ellen explained that they were going to be a group that included everyone and did special things for their fellow students—boys and girls—who might be sad or upset about something.

Mary Ellen already knew about a boy who was upset because his grandfather had died. She asked Susan and two of the original six girls to think of something that could cheer him up. They, including Susan, did. Susan said it made her feel good to have everyone not mad at her.

And no longer was Susan a bully. Mary Ellen is now thinking of her new plan.

1. Did Mary Ellen exhibit leadership through the symbolic frame?

Handout 39, Continued.

2. If she did, in what ways? If not, why not?

3. If not, how would Mary Ellen handle a bullying problem using the symbolic frame?

4. What do you believe her new plan will be?

Lesson 40

Fine Arts

Teacher's Note. The activity will require more time than one class period.

Objectives

In this lesson, students will:

- ◆ tap their ability as a leader using the symbolic frame, and
- ◆ utilize their understanding of the symbolic frame to research using different types of artistic media and theatre arts, including writing scripts and designing props.

Guiding Questions

- ◆ How does a person using the symbolic frame create a group activity?
- ◆ How does the leader using the symbolic frame facilitate group planning?

Materials

- ◆ Technology or paper to write scripts
- ◆ Variety of materials to create props
- ◆ Crayons, colored pencils, or other writing utensils for students
- ◆ Whiteboard, flipchart, or SmartBoard for discussion

Getting Ready

This activity incorporates creative thinking with skills of the symbolic frame. It may be used as an ongoing activity that students work on long-term. Remind students to reflect on how a person using the symbolic frame would offer leadership.

DOI:10.4324/9781003236122-45

Activity[1]

1. Say to students: *A color has disappeared. Your job involves researching the meanings, roles, and uses of colors to present a story about how the disappearance of a color changes the world. Along with your story, create a colorful character that is involved with the color's disappearance. Learn about and use technical theater methods to create the color's vanishing act. Present your story through a play or any product of your choice. Be ready to tell how using the symbolic frame facilitates the development of this activity.*

2. **Talk about it:** Discuss with students how using the symbolic frame helped in their research, the development of their character, and the vanishing act.

Assessment

Evaluate students' work using a rubric that fits your students' needs (see Lesson 3 for suggested resources).

Variation

Join Destination Imagination to find other creative activities that encourage students through technical, scientific, engineering, and fine arts challenges: https://www.destinationimagination.org.

---

1   *Note.* This activity was adapted from *2016–17 Fine Arts Challenge: Vanished!* [Video file], by Destination Imagination, 2016, retrieved from https://www.destinationimagination.org/blog/fine-arts-challenge-color-your-world-creative. Copyright 2016 by Destination Imagination. Adapted with permission.

Chapter 5

Leader Stories and Culminating Activity

Throughout history, stories have been used to share, interpret, and even shape experiences. Stories allow us to gain perspective and to digest information more easily. Through stories, people process, synthesize, and apply knowledge more deeply. By studying leaders past and present, other people learn from their experiences. The successes and failures of great leaders inspire, challenge, and, most importantly, provide insights that can change lives.

Analyzing leader stories through Bolman and Deal's (2014) frames—structural, human resource, political, and symbolic—helps deepen understanding and awareness and increase the ability to think in new ways to solve problems. Although most leaders have a natural tendency to lean into a particular strength resulting from their unique experiences and innate temperament and style, intentional leaders strengthen their ability to successfully identify and apply the most effective approach. This book is based on the premise that all leaders are more effective when they move outside of preferences and successfully apply other frames. Exploring others' stories and becoming skilled at identifying the frames leaders use to meet challenges and influence others improve the ability to exercise intentional leadership.

Four stories about real leaders follow; two are based on research (Castro, Parker), and two are based on in-person interviews (Hargrove, Schwartz). In each vignette, the leader's philosophy and strategy for meeting a challenge he or she faced is rooted in one or more of Bolman and Deal's (2014) frames. The stories allow students to demonstrate recognition and application of knowledge of the frames. In each story, one particular frame may stand out, but in all cases, elements of multiple frames are present. After each story, a set of questions provides a guide for student discussion. Finally, at the end of this chapter an exercise guides students to discover, share, and analyze their own selected leader stories.

 DOI:10.4324/9781003236122-46

Julian Castro: Man in the Crowd

At an early age, Julian Castro witnessed firsthand the importance of connecting with people to influence and effect change. His mother, Rosie, was an active community organizer in San Antonio during the Chicano movement in the 1960s and 70s. He and his twin brother, Joaquin, grew up attending local rallies, parades, and political functions with a front row view of grassroots efforts. His early career in local government strengthened his commitment to a "close-to-the ground" philosophy that has remained a hallmark of his leadership in all positions he has held (Kroll, 2015).

Castro served as the youngest person elected to the San Antonio City Council. After a first bid for the office of San Antonio Mayor was unsuccessful, he worked to build relationships with business leader, and hired his previous opponent's campaign team to run his campaign. He won in a landslide (Kroll, 2015). Among his accomplishments as a three-term mayor, Castro created a community-wide visioning project in which citizens set goals based on their collective vision for the city. He also led a voter referendum to expand Pre-Kindergarten education by rallying the critical support of key business leaders.

In 2014, Julian Castro was tapped by President Barack Obama to serve as secretary of the U.S. Department of Housing and Urban Development (HUD). In this role, he was responsible for 8,000 employees and a budget of more than $46 billion. As a leader, he described himself as a "man in the crowd," valuing being close to employees in order to understand the challenges and opportunities they face and what needs to be done better (Fox, 2014).

As the new leader of HUD, he had the opportunity to turn his philosophy into action. He soon faced the reality of his department repeatedly ranking low in the "Best Places to Work in the Federal Government." To address this problem, Castro leaned into his success in connecting with people and providing them with an opportunity to contribute their insights. He set out to improve communications to keep employees in the loop, increase engagement, and solicit feedback through frequent e-mails and newsletters, and by maintaining a visible presence with employees (Fox, 2014).

Castro's success—at all stops—was and is enhanced by his commitment to knowing people and creating opportunities for people to develop their strengths and participate actively in the process.

Discussion Questions

- ◆ Which frames are most recognizable in Julian Castro's leadership philosophy?
- ◆ What keywords or explanations led you to this conclusion?
- ◆ How might his early experiences influence his approach to situations?
- ◆ When faced with the challenges of losing an election and improving HUD, which frames did he use?

♦ How might he balance his natural leadership preferences through the development of the other frames?

Pauline Hargrove: Live a Great Story

Walk the halls of any of the six campuses in the Little Cypress-Mauriceville (LCM) CISD, and you'll quickly notice an abundance of individually decorated hard hats proudly displayed by faculty and staff. If you listen closely, you will hear the phrase "building excellence" being spoken in conversations between teachers, administrators, staff, and students. This is the districtwide message and theme for the school year, introduced to faculty and staff in poignant and dramatic fashion by Dr. Pauline Hargrove, superintendent of schools, at the annual convocation ceremony that marks the beginning of a new year. The hard hats are a tangible reminder of the year's focus, but also serve as a tool to draw people back to the big picture as challenges, celebrations, and opportunities for growth occur throughout the year.

For nearly 20 years, Hargrove has rallied school district employees, students, and the community around an annual focus point that is woven into the fabric of everything she does. Anticipating, embracing, and eagerly integrating the multilayered theme has become an integral part of the organization's culture. From hard hats to fishing lures to drums, she has effectively used stories, tokens, and a comprehensive message to unite, motivate, and inspire others into action.

To manage a complex operation like a school district, Hargrove acknowledges the importance of establishing detailed processes and procedures to guide employees. But what drives everything for her is a core belief that when people are valued as human beings and know that they are loved and respected, they can achieve their full potential. She works to build trust so others are able and willing to take risks, grow, and try new things. Her leadership goes beyond systems; through stories and themes Hargrove is building connections and creating an environment where those she serves will experience the power of their own story.

From a young age, Hargrove was taught the value of stories and traditions by her mother and father. Tales were often used to explore the habits, choices, and consequences in others' stories, which helped her to better understand her own. Throughout her life, she had an innate ability to compose and tell stories and a gift for creativity. But she also had an early realization that her own story impacts others and that all of our stories are interwoven; therefore, we have a responsibility to each other. As a classroom teacher, it was commonplace to see her students acting out a play she had written to help teach a lesson. As an elementary principal, she broadened this approach to lead an entire campus along a common path. When she made the transition to high school principal, some felt she would experience resistance to her approach—surely high school teachers and students would be less likely to respond.

But, Hargrove stayed true to her authentic self and successfully adapted her gifts to the high school environment. As it turned out, the deeper message of individual value resonated regardless of the method.

Over her 44-year career in education, Hargrove has effectively used creative themes and relevant stories to inspire people to connect with the district, each other, and most importantly, themselves. Although the themes, tokens, and messages change each year, the culture of creating and embracing meaningful, comprehensive messaging is apparent across the school district. In fact, if you ask someone about the "LC-M way," they will quickly respond with "Loving, Caring, and Motivating." These tenets lay the foundation for all to discover their own story, support each other, and achieve excellence. And by creating, nurturing, and sustaining this culture, Pauline Hargrove truly lives her own great story.

Discussion Questions

- ◆ Which frames are most recognizable in Pauline Hargrove's leadership strategy?
- ◆ What keywords or explanations led you to this conclusion?
- ◆ How might her early experiences influence her approach to situations?
- ◆ When she faced the challenge of working with different groups, did she apply a different frame? What may have contributed to her success?
- ◆ What are the possible positive or negative outcomes of the approaches you've identified?

Quanah Parker: From Warrior to Peacemaker

For more than 200 years, the Comanche Indians were the most notable tribe of the Southern Plains. Skilled horsemen and formidable warriors, they dominated large portions of present-day Texas, Colorado, New Mexico, Oklahoma, and Kansas. In the 1800s, U.S. settlers began to move across Texas and into Comanche territory, and the Comanche fought fiercely to protect and maintain their way of life.

The U.S. began efforts in the late 1860s to move the Comanche into reservations. A young warrior named Quanah led the last free band of the Comanche. Quanah was the son of a Comanche chief and Cynthia Ann Parker, a White settler who had been kidnapped as a child and assimilated into the tribe. As he watched his people's numbers decrease and as the Comanche's primary livelihood, the bison, were hunted to near extinction, Quanah finally surrendered and peacefully led his tribe to the reservation.

Although adjusting to a new world order was difficult for many Native Americans, Quanah keenly positioned himself to leverage key relationships and resources in order to gain influence. The federal government appointed him principal chief of the entire Comanche nation. He embraced many of the "White man's ways," including taking his mother's last name—thus becoming Quanah Parker. Over the next 25 years, he learned English, became a reservation judge, lobbied Congress, and pleaded the cause of the Comanche Nation.

Recognizing that resources were limited for his people, he formed relationships with Texas cattlemen like Charles Goodnight, business leaders, and even President Theodore Roosevelt. Through these coalitions, he negotiated grazing rights to secure payments for use of grazing on his tribe's land and even invested in a railroad. On the reservation, he encouraged self-sufficiency among his people through building schools, creating ranching operations, and planting crops (Weiser, 2010). Although he adapted and encouraged his tribe to do the same, he also worked to preserve the Comanche culture and traditions.

His efforts did not come without criticism. Although praised by many in his tribe, Parker was also criticized for what some saw as selling out to the White man by adapting and becoming a rancher. Others recognized that he did what was necessary to ensure survival and even prosperity for his people.

Biographer Bill Neeley (1996) wrote of Parker, "Not only did Quanah pass within the span of a single lifetime from a Stone Age warrior to a statesman in the age of the Industrial Revolution, but he accepted the challenge and responsibility of leading the whole Comanche tribe on the difficult road toward their new existence" (as cited in Famous Texans, n.d., para. 7). Quanah Parker led his people by maximizing resources and effectively transitioning from warrior to peacemaker.

Discussion Questions

- Which frames are most recognizable in Quanah Parker's leader story?
- What keywords or explanations led you to this conclusion?
- How did his experiences influence his approach to situations?
- How might he have applied other frames to address the challenges of leading his people through the transition to a reservation?
- What are the possible positive or negative outcomes of this approach?

Roberta Schwartz: The Power of the Plan

Who would have thought that a young candy striper working in a community hospital would one day be at the helm of a *U.S. News & World Report* Honor Roll Hospital and the top ranked hospital in Texas and the Gulf Coast? It is no surprise to anyone who knows Roberta Levy Schwartz, including Roberta. As a young volunteer, she knew she wanted to run a hospital one day, and she laid out a plan to gain experiences that would help her reach her goal. Today, Schwartz serves as executive vice president of The Methodist Hospital. In this role, she oversees the strategic direction and operations of a hospital that has had more national rankings than any other hospital in Texas for more than a decade. The Methodist Hospital, an 860-bed adult teaching hospital in Houston's Texas Medical Center, documents 39,000 annual admissions, 1,600 physicians, more than 6,000 employees, and a $1.5 billion budget.

It takes determination and deliberate planning to reach this level of leadership, but sustained success requires the ability to simultaneously build a strong team, recognize trends, and design and implement the right plan at the right time. When Roberta Schwartz was faced with a major budget challenge that, if not resolved, would affect thousands of employees and hospital services, the foundation she laid in these areas allowed the team to navigate the challenge successfully.

To lead an operation the size and scope of the hospital, the leadership team is critical. Schwartz surrounds herself with highly capable people who know their business inside and out. But she also stresses the importance of building a team with great diversity of opinions, with each member willing to share perspectives freely—even in disagreement. She nurtures this culture through a strong personal commitment to transparency and a consistent effort to demonstrate a sense of calm—a focus on not overreacting.

As a highly attuned leader, Schwartz constantly watches and listens to what is happening both inside and outside of the organization. As a result, she noticed trends occurring that could affect the hospital's budget and she initiated conversations to prepare for how she would lead her team to address the challenges. When the fear became a reality and she was faced with a $4 million shortfall, Schwartz did not panic. She leaned into her team, and together they crafted a detailed plan to recover.

Schwartz assembled her leadership team and facilitated a review of each department's budget and services. Her clearly stated goal for the team was to close the gap without enacting a reduction in staff. This detailed process required clearly set guidelines and specifically identified targets for savings. Over the next few months, team leaders engaged staff to realistically communicate what cuts would be fair and workable. The leadership team met often, followed the guidelines set, adjusted targets when necessary, and leaned into each other's expertise.

The result? In just a few months, the team made up the budget shortfall. Schwartz's ability to engage her team to design and execute a thorough plan allowed her to maintain staff positions and services.

Discussion Questions

- Which frames are most recognizable in Roberta Schwartz's primary leadership strategy?
- What keywords or explanations led you to this conclusion?
- How did her early experiences influence her approach to situations?
- In facing the budget crisis, how did she effectively blend frames to accomplish her goals?
- How might she have applied other frames to address this challenge?

Culminating Activity

Fascinating and instructive leader stories exist all around us. Leaders can benefit by developing the lifelong habit of studying leaders—their philosophies, challenges faced, successes, and failures. Analyzing leader stories and identifying the frames used by others—structural, human resource, political, and symbolic—enhances the ability to recognize when a situation calls for a specific frame and strengthens the ability to intentionally shift the approach to meet challenges and influence others.

This culminating activity, detailed on the handout on the following page, will help students synthesize the concepts covered in this book. It may also be used by educators to help develop additional leader stories that can be utilized with students to explore leadership frames.

By discovering, sharing, and analyzing leader stories, students will become skilled at identifying the frames leaders use to meet challenges and influence others. This habit will improve their ability to exercise intentional leadership.

Culminating Activity

Directions: Choose a leader whose story inspires, challenges, or provides you with an important insight. This leader story can focus on someone from history or a current leader you read about—a political leader, a successful business leader, or perhaps a social activist. Or maybe this is someone you know personally—a school leader such as an administrator, a community leader, a local business leader, or a church leader. Whether you research this person or you conduct an in-person interview, ask or seek answers to the following questions:

- ◆ What does being a leader mean to you?
- ◆ What are the key characteristics that shape your leadership style?
- ◆ How would others describe your leadership strategies?
- ◆ How do you organize and motivate people you are charged with leading?
- ◆ Describe a challenge you faced as a leader. How did you resolve the situation?
- ◆ What were the outcomes (positive and/or negative)?

Once you have the answers to these questions (and maybe others you develop), write your leader story. Great stories include three parts: the set up, the confrontation, and the resolution. Think about organizing your story this way. The set up might involve background information or an explanation of the leader's philosophy. The confrontation centers on the challenge he or she faced. The resolution shows how the challenge was addressed and any outcomes (positive or negative).

Now, analyze your leader's story through the lens of the four frames. Which frame is most natural for this leader? What makes you think this way? What frame did the leader apply to his or her challenge? Was it the same frame as his or her "preferred style"? What frame should this leader work to develop?

References

Bass, B. M., & Stogdill, R. M. (1990). *Bass & Stogdill's handbook of leadership: Theory, research, and managerial applications* (3rd ed.). New York, NY: Free Press.

Bennis, W. G., & Townsend, R. (2005). *Reinventing leadership: Strategies to empower the organization.* New York, NY: HarperCollins.

Bolman, L. G., & Deal. T. E. (2014). *How great leaders think: The art of reframing.* Hoboken, NJ: Wiley.

Brown, B. (2012). *Leadership series: Vulnerability and inspired leadership* [Web log post]. Retrieved from http://www.impatientoptimists.org/Posts/2012/11/Leadership-Series-Vulnerability-and-Inspired-Leadership

Burns, J. M. (1978). *Leadership.* New York, NY: Harper & Row.

Collins, J. (2001). *Good to great: Why some companies make the leap . . . and others don't.* New York, NY: HarperCollins.

Covey, S. (2004). *The 8th habit: From effectiveness to greatness.* New York, NY: Free Press.

Destination Imagination. (2016). *2016–17 fine arts challenge: Vanished!* [Video file]. Retrieved from https://www.destinationimagination.org/blog/fine-arts-challenge-color-your-world-creative

Famous Texans. (n.d.). *Quanah Parker.* Retrieved from http://www.famoustexans.com/quanahparker.htm

Fox, T. (2014). Julian Castro shares his thoughts on leadership. *The Washington Post.* Retrieved from https://www.washingtonpost.com/news/on-leadership/wp/2014/12/18/julian-castro-shares-his-thoughts-on-leadership

Giles, S. (2016). The most important leadership competencies, according to leaders around the world. *Harvard Business Review.* Retrieved from https://hbr.org/2016/03/the-most-important-leadership-competencies-according-to-leaders-around-the-world

Greenleaf, R. K. (1979). *Servant leadership: A journey into the nature of legitimate power and greatness*. New York, NY: Paulist Press.

Hurt, P. L. (2013). *JJ did tie buckle: Learn the leadership traits to the United States Marines*. Seattle, WA: CreateSpace.

Karnes, F. A., & Bean, S. M. (2010). *Leadership for students: A guide for young leaders* (2nd ed.). Waco, TX: Prufrock Press.

Kirkpatrick, S. A., & Locke, E. A. (1991). Leadership: Do traits matter? *Academy of Management Executive, 5*(2), 48–60.

Kouzes, J. M., & Posner, B. Z. (1995). *The leadership challenge: How to get things done in organizations*. San Francisco, CA: Jossey-Bass.

Kroll, A. (2015). The power of two: Inside the rise of the Castro brothers. *The Atlantic*. Retrieved from https://www.theatlantic.com/politics/archive/2015/01/the-power-of-two-inside-the-rise-of-the-castro-brothers/440034

Leshnower, S. (2008). Teaching leadership. *Gifted Child Today, 31*(2), 29–35.

Marland, S. P., Jr. (1972). *Education of the gifted and talented: Report to the Congress of the United States by the U.S. Commissioner of Education and background papers submitted to the U.S. Office of Education*, 2 vols. Washington, DC: U.S. Government Printing Office. (Government Documents Y4.L 11/2: G36)

Maslow, A. H. (1954). *Motivation and personality*. New York, NY: Harper & Brothers.

Matthews, M. S. (2004). Leadership education for gifted and talented youth: A review of the literature. *Journal for the Education of Gifted, 28*, 77–112.

National Association for Gifted Children. (2010). *Redefining giftedness for a new century: Shifting the paradigm* [Position paper]. Washington, DC: Author.

Neeley, B. (1996). *The last Comanche chief: The life and times of Quanah Parker*. New York, NY: Wiley & Sons.

Nelson, A. E. (2016). *The O factor: Identifying and developing students gifted in leadership ability*. Fort Collins, CO: Summit Crest.

Pink, D. H. (2006). *A whole new mind: Why right-brainers will rule the world*. New York, NY: Penguin.

Prive, T. (2012). Top 10 qualities that make a great leader. *Forbes*. Retrieved from http://www.forbes.com/sites/tanyaprive/2012/12/19/top-10-qualities-that-make-a-great-leader

Revised Texas Education Code 29.D. §29.121 (1995), Education Program for Gifted and Talented Students: Definition.

Rohnke, K., & Butler, S. (1995). *Quicksilver: Adventure games, initiative problems, trust activities and a guide to effective leadership*. Beverly, MA: Project Adventure.

Sandberg, S. (2013). *Lean in: Women, work, and the will to lead*. New York, NY: Random House.

Title V, Part D. [Jacob K. Javits Gifted and Talented Students Education Act of 1988], Elementary and Secondary Education Act of 1988 (2002), 20 U.S.C. sec. 7253 et seq.

Weiser, K. (2010). Native American legends: Quanah Parker: Last chief of the Comanche. *Legends of America*. Retrieved from http://www.legendsofamerica.com/na-quanahparker.html

About the Authors

Cecelia Boswell, Ed.D., is an educator with more than 40 years of experience as teacher, consultant, auditor for G/T and IB, a director of advanced academics, and past-president of the Texas Association for the Gifted and Talented (TAGT) and the Council for Exceptional Children, The Association for Gifted (CEC-TAG). She has coauthored four books and is currently working with districts throughout Texas auditing G/T and IB.

Mary Christopher, Ph.D., taught gifted children for many years prior to becoming a professor of educational studies at Hardin-Simmons University in 1996. She serves as program director of the Masters in Gifted Education and Doctorate in Leadership programs at HSU. She also works as an educational consultant in gifted education, leadership, and strategic planning. She served as board member and past-president of TAGT.

JJ Colburn, M.Ed., CAE, serves as president and partner at Strategic Association Management in Austin, TX. He was previously the executive director of TAGT, has served as the director of the Texas Association of Student Councils, and is a former social studies teacher, counselor, and student leadership consultant and trainer. He is a director in the Texas Lyceum and has served as Board Chairman of the Texas Society of Association Executives.